RAISA

The 1st First Lady
of the Soviet Union

by URDA JÜRGENS

TRANSLATED BY SYLVIA CLAYTON

SUMMIT BOOKS
New York • London • Toronto • Sydney • Tokyo • Singapore

SUMMIT BOOKS
Simon & Schuster Building
Rockefeller Center
1230 Avenue of the Americas
New York, New York 10020

10 9 8 7 6 5 4 3 2 1

Library of Congress Cataloging in Publication Data

Jürgens, Urda.
  [Raissa Gorbatschowa. English]
  Raisa, the 1st first lady of the Soviet Union / by Urda
Jürgens ; translated by Sylvia Clayton.
     p.   cm.
  Translation of: Raissa Gorbatschowa.
  Includes index.
  1.Gorbacheva, Raisa Maksimova. 2.Heads of state—
Soviet Union—Wives—Biography. 3.Soviet Union—
Politics and government—1985–
I.Title.
DK290.3.G675J8713   1990
947.085'4—dc20
[B]   91-8234
                                                            CIP
ISBN 0-671-72663-3

 # Contents

PART ONE

Introduction

WHILE SHE WAS being briefed for one of her many meetings with Raisa Gorbachev, Nancy Reagan made a surprising discovery. She was told by protocol officials that in the Russian language there is no expression for "First Lady." True, the Soviet Union had women coal miners, road builders, and electrical engineers. But even seventy years after the Revolution, some things hadn't changed. As in the days of the tsars, women were expected to play a subordinate role—like children, to be seen but not heard. A Soviet "First Lady"? An alien notion, unthinkable.

What there had been in the upper circles of the Soviet regime were gray, anonymous wives. It is hard to forget the image of Nina Khrushchev at the summit in Vienna in 1961—clumsy and awkward, sitting next to a radiantly smiling Jacqueline Kennedy. Or Yuri Andropov's wife—Western journalists didn't even know that the previous General Secretary had a wife until Gorbachev, on Russian television, endeavored to comfort her at her husband's funeral. Even in *Pravda,* the country's leading newspaper, pictures of top officials' wives rarely appeared, and when they did, they remained unidentified. Television announcers simply ignored their unfamiliar presence on the screen. In fact, during one of Gorbachev's early visits to Washington, when asked by an American reporter what the plans were for covering Raisa a Soviet reporter replied, "That's your problem. We don't write about her."

They do now, not only because of the role she has created but because of the kind of woman she is—educated, charming, attractive (she works out with American exercise tapes), and articulate. During an early trip to London she dazzled journalists with her command of English language and literature. One group of photographers was so impressed that they bought her a bouquet—and that was in 1984, before her husband even assumed the General Secretary post.

Raisa Gorbachev is but one reflection of the modern, progressive style that her husband has introduced to the Soviet Union. Not since Nadezhda Krupskaya, the wife to whom Lenin attributed all his best thoughts, has there been a woman so prominent in Soviet political life. It takes a strong woman to fill that role which no one doubts Raisa is. She is also intelligent, ambitious, accomplished (she is the first among Kremlin wives—or U.S. presidents' wives, for that matter—to hold a Ph.D.), and, more important, a woman who clearly relishes her public role. It wasn't only that Nina Khrushchev wasn't slim or elegant or fashionably dressed, but that she was uncomfortable in the spotlight. No one can say that about Raisa. "Misha, Misha," onlookers often hear her saying in her "pay attention" voice to summon her husband, who likes to chat informally with journalists. But if she enjoys her public role, it is one that has brought her as much criticism at home as it has adulation abroad. "First Lady" is a new phenomenon to the Russians, and not an entirely welcome one.

"Soviet Realism's answer to Princess Diana," the English say; a "one-woman Revolution," trumpets *Time* magazine. But at home, the epithets are far different: "Little Empress," "Tsarina," she has been called. Some detractors even wear buttons: "Raisa Nyet." The reasons vary, but many have economic roots. Western women like Raisa's outfits, but for most Russian women, Raisa's polished looks and lifestyle are beyond their reach. Women in factories or on collective farms who meet her in her travels are likely to look on her with envy. She is too remote from the people, they complain, and her priorities are all wrong: she's too much the queen and too little the wife. And where could they find such outfits? Even in the biggest stores in Moscow, the clothes Raisa wears, the jewels she buys, aren't available to them. There is one story about the Gorbachevs' visit to a certain town where women with only two dresses in their entire wardrobe commented sardonically on the fact that during the brief visit Raisa changed her outfit twice.

For the opposition, Raisa's finery—excessive only in Soviet terms—makes for good political artillery. Reportedly, a secret videotape in Moscow shows Raisa buying jewelry with an American Express Gold Card in London. (American Express refuses to answer whether the Gorbachevs are "card-carriers.") Gorbachev's allies naturally attribute the tape to his enemies, but its existence, or even its rumored existence, indicates the hostility Raisa has aroused and the potential liability this sophisticated First Lady has become.

Not all the negativity is limited to Russia. Nancy Reagan apparently wasn't too fond of Raisa during the summit meeting of 1987. There was their famous tour of the White House, during which Mrs. Gorbachev peppered a flustered Mrs. Reagan with questions, the answers to many of which she didn't know (like, "When was the White House built?"). In retaliation, Mrs. Reagan's staff let it seep out after the tour that Mrs.

Gorbachev's dress was "a bit too cocktailish" and made
reference to her baggy hose. "Who does that dame think
she is?" Mrs. Reagan reportedly said. Obviously, the
karma wasn't good. In her memoir, *My Turn,* Nancy
Reagan calls Raisa Gorbachev "arrogant" and accuses
her of a conversational style that made her "bristle." But
Mrs. Gorbachev gets along a lot better with Mrs.
Reagan's successor, Barbara Bush. During her 1990
visit, the American press reported gleefully that Raisa
"bonded" with Millie, the First Lady's First Dog, and
was even surprised to note that on one occasion, Mrs.
Gorbachev gave Mrs. Bush a recipe for a berry dessert—
allowing a rare glimpse of her domestic side.

All these incidents and opinions add up to a con-
flicting portrait of Raisa Gorbachev, a woman admired
by her international audience and the younger generation at home but lambasted by her husband's peers.
Who is Raisa Gorbachev, really?

It is hard for a stranger to know. The trouble with
writing a biography of any Soviet citizen is that the
Communist Party, at least in the past, tended to san-
itize official facts. And to get unofficial facts was risky.
Still, in the current atmosphere of *glasnost,* there are
friends and colleagues who are willing to talk, though
usually with restraint. Lydia Budyka, a pediatrician, is
one of Raisa's closest friends, but she was willing to
talk only under certain conditions: following each interview, she had to refer back to Raisa. Sometimes
Mrs. Gorbachev wasn't available, other times the message would come back that Raisa didn't want a certain
fact or photograph published at all. People who spoke
with fewer restrictions also tended to be less candid.
Their accounts were often glowing, though this by itself is not necessarily proof that they weren't saying
what they felt. They might simply have felt defensive
with the foreign press.

Because of the handicaps in researching any Soviet

biography, then, even in the time of Gorbachev, this account may leave questions unanswered, paradoxes unresolved. I hope, if it explains only one fact, it explains why, of all the potential Russian First Ladies, it is Raisa Gorbachev who was first.

ONE

The Railway Child

THE RUSSIANS like to use diminutives instead of full names. The name recorded on the birth certificate is generally used only when the person concerned is in some kind of trouble, which is why so many Russians go through life without ever being called by their actual first name: Maria becomes Maya, Mikhail turns into Misha. On January 5, 1932, Shura Paradina, wife of Maxim Titorenko, gave birth to their first child. But even before the end of her first year, her name, Raisa Maximovna Titorenko, had been softened to Raya.

Little is known of Raisa's distant ancestry. Her grandparents on her mother's side kept a small shop in the tiny town of Vessolayarsk in western Siberia. There wasn't much you could buy in this remote part of Russia, but what you could was that in that shop. The family, though hardly prosperous, had enough to feed their children, perhaps even give them a taste for something more. It is a taste that their daughter, Shura Paradina, evidently acquired.

She was eighteen when she met Maxim, twenty-six, a railway worker from Tishemilov in the Ukraine. His previous job had been at Lokot, building freight trains for the town of Ridder, which, like so many Russian towns, had been rechristened after the Revolution. Now, it was Leninogorsk. By all accounts, Shura was a cheerful, vivacious and resolute young woman, and Maxim fell in love. They were married in typical post-Revolution style: everything was done modestly in those difficult times. Primarily, the guests indulged in sentiment.

Not long after they were married, Shura became pregnant. Maxim was understandably nervous in anticipating his first child. Vessolayarsk had no hospital or even a midwife, and the snows of January would make traveling a slow and risky ordeal. When her time drew near, Maxim drove Shura in a trap to Rubtsovsk, a town with a hospital eighteen miles away. Braving the ice and cold in her ninth month of pregnancy could not have been easy for Shura, but ease was not a fact of life in rural Russia. Its absence is what makes inhabitants of this part of Russia strong. And Shura was of that breed.

Shura came home healthy and content, and happy about her new baby. Raisa was a beautiful and active child, with deep brown eyes and coppery hair. The winter of 1932 was exceptionally severe, but Raisa grew sturdily through her first year, confirming another Russian folk belief, that the healthiest children are those who have to battle harsh weather in the early months of their lives.

Vessolayarsk was an unlovely little town in the Altai Mountains less than four hundred miles from the borders of China and Mongolia. It was a melting pot of languages and cultures, and far from the influences of cosmopolitan Moscow and the Europeanized west.

The key fact about Vessolayarsk, however, was its location in Siberia, whose name at once implies beauty— the never-ending plains, the great forests, nature untouched and unspoiled—and death. Even in the time of the tsars, Siberia was considered a place to die. The Russians described it as their "biggest prison," and successive rulers made use of it for just that, though it was under Stalin that the art of banishment reached its peak. Siberia was home for people who opposed authority but also for exiles and fugitives, people without papers who had managed to escape from the bureaucratic or penal clutches of the Communist Party. Siberia, the locals said, either killed you or set you free.

Except for the natural ones, the privations of Siberia did not affect Raisa as a child. She lived in Vessolayarsk for two more or less uneventful years, while her father continued to work for the railroad. Working under a quota system and not for a fixed salary, he could stop working only when the day's chores were done, often resulting in a twelve-hour day. And he was also required to make frequent trips away from home.

But Maxim's job brought privileges as well. In so vast a land, Russians have always been dependent on their railroads. Even today with widespread air service, the railroads are still regarded as the arteries of the USSR: block them and the whole country breaks down. The Soviets were conscious of this from the outset, and the social status of the railway worker was given an official boost. In their writings, the intelligentsia were instructed to exalt the railway worker, lifting what was often grimy and backbreaking work to a noble plane. As a result, railway workers received a higher than average salary and were given a modest wooden house. They were among the first workers granted an annual holiday and were second, after civil servants, to receive a retirement pension. Consequently, even among the working class, they formed a privileged brigade. And they had one other advantage: a uniform. In a country where clothes were of such poor quality and in short supply, a uniform, alone, lent a measure of status.

The Titorenko family enjoyed these amenities and considered themselves privileged. But there was a price to pay: their life was constantly disrupted by the needs of the state. Even in peacetime, railway workers were at the mercy of national goals, military or otherwise. Consequently, Maxim had to work where he was sent, sometimes with his family and sometimes alone.

In 1934, when Raisa was two, her brother Evgeny was born. That same year, Maxim was transferred to Chernigov in the Ukraine and took his family with him. Chernigov was practically on the other side of the world, 1,800 miles from Vessolayarsk, which meant Raisa had to leave her grandparents, with whom she was very close. The disruption was especially painful for Shura, who had come to depend on her parents during Maxim's frequent trips away from home. Despite the arrival of her second child, Shura continued to work full time in her job as a railway inspector, only now she didn't have her parents to help her through difficult times. As for money, Maxim's salary wasn't low: between 750 and 800 rubles a month in the 1930s. They could afford the basic necessities, even a bottle of vodka once in a while, but not much more. Shura could not afford to give up her job. Her children received whatever free time was left.

But if the economic realities under Stalin were hard, the political ones were even worse. Throughout the 1930s, the OGPU, the Soviet secret police, arrested not only those who criticized the regime but those they suspected of harboring such thoughts. Imprisonment spread over the nation like a wave. By the mid-1930s some 16 million people were in Stalinist labor camps, and many of them never made it out. In 1935 Maxim Titorenko joined the ranks of the victimized. Raisa was three when her father was arrested and banished to a prison camp. His offense: speaking on the dire economic and political consequences of the forced collectivization of agriculture. (Though difficult to verify, it is rumored that Maxim Titorenko was an associate of Lenin's in several economic experiments in the 1920s. As such, he might have had passionate feelings about the way the rural economy was being mismanaged.)

Through both luck and Shura's fortitude, life was not as difficult for the family as it might have been while Maxim was in prison. Unlike the families of other prisoners, the Titorenkos were not thrown out into the street. Though their house was confiscated, they were given a smaller one in which to live. There was no electricity and no running water, but Shura, as resourceful as the situation demanded, managed to make it livable. She divided the small space into thirds: a bedroom, a bathroom, and a parlor-kitchen, the centerpiece of which was a stove. With Maxim gone, at least she could feed her children and keep them warm.

But they did suffer. These years were marked by anxiety, insecurity, and bouts of dismal poverty. Raisa was forced to take on great responsibilities. There was baby brother Evgeny to help care for and a household to tend. Her mother, that strong and stoical woman, even she occasionally broke down, weeping over her loneliness and the injustice of her husband's plight. Now, especially, Shura missed her parents, but travel, except at the highest levels, was prohibited for the families of prisoners. Far from anyone they knew or cared about, the Titorenkos, once a typical extended family, now had only themselves on whom to depend.

Despite the precariousness of their life, Shura strived to give her family a sense of security and well-being. "She made us clothes, she cooked, she sang little songs, she was there, and we felt protected," Raisa said in one of her few public comments about her mother. Shura also made sure that her children were well trained. "We used to go mushrooming, collecting them and drying them. Our mother really watched over us and insisted on a certain amount of discipline, which was soon of value to us."

In many positive ways, Raisa's friend Lydia Budyka observed, Raisa resembles her mother. "Her mother is intelligent and full of energy. Although she is not highly educated, she is extremely perceptive." As for her father, his impression on her was fainter, and the memories bittersweet. "He was a shy man, quiet, friendly, and very tenderhearted," Budyka said. "Raisa was greatly attached to him and often wept for him when he was in the prison camp."

After four years of imprisonment, Maxim Titorenko was released from the Solovetski labor camp and returned to his family. Prison life had weakened him physically, but in other ways he emerged a more enlightened man. Barely educated when he left, he was able to take advantage of the one opportunity a Stalinist prison camp afforded: to mingle with some of the most inspired thinkers of the day. Among these was his close friend and cellmate, Dmitri Likhachev, a devoted student of the arts. Likhachev, too, had been arrested for speaking freely—in his case, against the squandering of Russia's cultural resources and the shameful neglect of its rich artistic past. Through late-night discussions and soliloquies at work, Likhachev passed along much of his knowledge to his friend. For the humble railway worker, it was a middle-aged renaissance.

Over the next fifty years, Likhachev would become a respected leader in Soviet artistic and cultural life. He was one of the founders of the Soviet government's Cultural Foundation, to whose board he appointed the daughter of his old prison-mate, Raisa Gorbachev. She, in turn, supported his goal of encouraging Soviet cultural life. Even in America, Likhachev became known, albeit briefly. When Nancy Reagan toured Leningrad's Hermitage Museum in 1988, it was this "revered scholar," according to U.S. newspapers, who showed her around.

Titorenko's return, in 1939, coincided with Raisa's first year of school and the beginning of World War II, but the reality of the war was yet to be strongly felt in Russia. Despite Hitler's ruthless invasion of Poland, the people felt relatively secure: the Hitler-Stalin pact would guarantee them peace.

Nonetheless, by autumn 1939, a massive relocation of Soviet industries had begun. Giant armament factories were set up in the Ural Mountains and whole establishments were shifted east. One train after another rumbled out of the Ukraine and western Russia to new production centers in Siberia. As a railway family, the Titorenkos were forced to move, too—many times, in fact, to wherever the government saw fit. In those years, Raisa's schools read like a series of stops on the Soviet rail map: town after anonymous town, changing so rapidly their identities seemed to merge in her mind. Educationally, she did not suffer—Soviet schools conformed rigidly to one curriculum—but emotionally, it was a terrible strain. She and her brother were constantly having to adjust to new friends, classes, and teachers. The family's itinerant life was perhaps one reason why, as a child, she was thought to be extremely shy and, as a young woman, reserved. Just as she began to make new friends, it would be time to pack up and leave. Even when they stayed, their life had a quality of impermanence. Nothing illustrates this better than the kind of house in which they frequently lived: a spare railway wagon which was simply hitched to a locomotive when it was time to leave.

Raisa's student career began with the compulsory four years of primary school. The Soviet school system, though advanced in many ways, was socially conservative: boys and girls together in the first two grades, but not beyond. The curriculum at Raisa's tiny school (only thirty pupils) consisted of math, Russian language and literature, drawing, singing, and physical education.

Language and literature were Raisa's favorites. Even

before primary school, she had been taught the value of reading. Here, too, her inspiration was Shura. Only minimally educated, like Maxim, Shura understood the value of reading as the process through which one learned. Reading built character, she said. When things didn't come easily to Raisa, Shura was there to make sure she persevered.

In 1940, Raisa's sister, Ludmilla, was born. This placed an additional burden on Raisa, as Shura continued to work full-time. As best she could, Shura divided her time between work and family, but the strain was great, a fact that wasn't lost on her elder daughter, who in later years wrote about this dilemma faced by all Soviet mothers.

Any illusions that had been fostered by the Hitler-Stalin pact were abruptly shattered in 1941, with Hitler's three-pronged invasion of Russia. The great peacemaker, Comrade Stalin, was now the great leader of the Soviet people's gallant war efforts. "Everything for the Front" was the new rallying cry. Raisa had only been in school for two years when again her life was disrupted. Mobilizing for the Great Patriotic War created enormous upheavals as goods and services disappeared from the domestic economy and were channeled to the front. The Titorenkos endured greatly reduced circumstances, and both parents were driven to the point of physical exhaustion. Naturally, Raisa felt the fallout of all this stress.

Amid such hardship, school was her salvation. She was, from the start, an ideal student. Books, especially, provided the beauty and comfort that the war years did not, and unlike the adventures of her everyday life, the ones described in literature were magnificently unreal. There were other outlets, too. Like many children her age, she was given her first taste of political education through membership in the Young Pioneers. A children's organization founded in Lenin's time, the Young Pioneers were in some respects a Soviet equivalent of the Boy Scouts or Girl Scouts, but with a decidedly political tone. Under Stalin, however, it became even more political and in a rather treacherous way. A ministerial decree published in 1943 sought to strengthen its ties to the party and use it as a propaganda machine. Its goal: to foment passionate hatred of the so-called enemies of the Russian people.

Members enthusiastically recited the Young Pioneer motto (which is not quite as lyrical in translation):

> *When you put on your Pioneer scarf*
> *You must guard it*
> *It has the same red color*
> *As our country's flag.*

Every morning they had to repeat the Young Pioneer greeting, a more militaristic pledge of allegiance: "On with the struggle for the cause of Lenin and Stalin, be ready. Always ready." The red scarf, which members were taught to handle as reverently as the Communist Party card itself, bore the legend "Thank you, Comrade Stalin, for a happy childhood."

Raisa embodied the higher aspirations of the Young Pioneers, with her positive attitude toward learning, her diligence, and strength. And with so much upheaval in her life, she took comfort in both fitting in and standing out in such a favorable way. As for ideology, the politicization of the school system escalated under Stalin, and just as Raisa was a product of her mother's strength and her father's suffering, she was also a product of her Stalin-inspired youth.

In 1943, Raisa entered secondary school in Krasnodar. Here, the curriculum broadened to include history, geography, botany, zoology, foreign languages and, in the final year, psychology, a strange addition given the strictures of Stalinist thought. But socially, the environment became more strict. Girls had to wear uniforms;

elaborate hairdos and cosmetics were banned. Innovation was discouraged and uniformity stressed at the expense of personal growth.

This repressive atmosphere left little room for the creative development of the child. At different times, reformers recognized the consequences of such a rigid system, but they were defeated by the growing party bureaucracy, which tightened its grip on every sphere of life. School demanded total obedience and total discipline. But it was politically that the system manifested its most repressive side. Pictures of "revolutionaries" who had been purged by Stalin were either blotted out with ink or mysteriously excised from textbooks. Sometimes, only the eyes were scissored out.

But even the most enlightened parents dared not complain. Maxim Titorenko and his family had already experienced firsthand the terrors of the Stalin period. Now, they too yielded to the politics of quietism. Under Stalin, to be unobtrusive was to survive.

The school system had positive aspects as well, among them academic rigor. Courses were demanding, examinations tough. In such an atmosphere, a diligent student like Raisa could be expected to thrive. It behooved the ambitious student to learn as much as possible about Stalin, which posed no great difficulty given his ubiquity. Pictures of the dictator were everywhere: on the walls, in newspapers, on posters in the street. People viewed him with fear, but also with reverence: he was their terrible but respected leader who, in telling them that he was great, bequeathed his greatness to them. In making himself a god, he made them his chosen people. And where such an attitude didn't come naturally, it was enforced. In every essay she wrote, Raisa, like her comrades, praised Stalin. A good student did: the more glowing the praise, the higher the mark.

Raisa was thirteen when the war ended in 1945. More than the Americans, the French, or the English, the Russians suffered. As many as 20 million people died, the casualties evenly divided between military and civilian. The toll taken by starvation and frostbite was so great that about 55 percent of the casualties were women. Amid such wreckage, rebuilding the nation was naturally the theme. The new era brought peace but not prosperity, and like their countrymen, the Titorenkos struggled to recover. Between her household chores and caring for her siblings, Raisa hardly had a moment to breathe, but her mother made sure that there was always time for study. Shura vested her hopes in her bright and ambitious daughter, who, among her other abilities, according to her friend Lydia, was "keen on group projects" and "a natural leader even then."

Shura was not disappointed. At the end of tenth grade, Raisa was given the top mark, a 5, in every subject and passed all her exams with distinction. She managed to do equally well in the subsequent grades and graduated at the top of her class. Only one in a hundred graduates were awarded a gold medal; one in fifty, a silver one. Raisa won a gold medal, which qualified her automatically for admission to a university. Another criterion was correct political views, which, at her interview, Raisa proved she had too. Eventually, she was accepted at Moscow State University, which to her family was the realization of a dream. Not only was she the first member to be admitted to college, but to one as prestigious as Moscow State.

AT THE SAME TIME Raisa was attending school in a succession of villages, a peasant boy two years older than she was working the fields with his father in Privolnoye, a town too small to be found on most maps. The nearest large town was several hours away by foot and Stavropol, the regional capital, was at least a day's travel. The boy, the eldest son of Sergei Gorbachev, an agricultural worker, led a life not unlike his rural peers. His carefree childhood was short, ending as soon as he was old enough to work in the fields. From then on, his days were divided between school and work. The only difference a holiday made was that then he spent the whole day in the fields.

Like the Titorenkos before they left Vessolayarsk, the Gorbachevs had the benefit of an extended family. Children, grandparents, everyone worked in the fields and pitched in at home. Economically, the nuclear family made little sense in rural life. While Sergei Gorbachev served as a soldier during the war and his wife worked in another town, the family was presided over by the grandparents, with whom Mikhail, or Misha, as he was called, was extremely close.

The countryside where Misha spent most of his youth was unique in several ways. Historically on the frontiers of Russian imperialism, it was inhabited by Cossacks, free farmers who owed allegiance to no feudal lords. The richness of the land both encouraged their independence—they had to defend themselves from aggressive nomads—and gave them the means to retain it: the land was so rich that they could feed themselves and sell the surplus. Not surprisingly, the Cossacks were violently opposed to Communism, with its emphasis on state rather than individual control. Officials sent by the state to collectivize them in the 1920s and early '30s met with armed resistance.

Conditions in the Altai Mountains where Raisa was born were not so different. Despite the great distances between Altai and Stavropol, both were "territories" and naturally isolated, which gave their inhabitants a little extra breathing space—not unlike the American frontier. Here, historically, Russians found sanctuary from the police, army officials, and tax inspectors. Members of the Russian Orthodox Church also settled here but did not proselytize. People lived in harmony, even cooperatively, without any help from the state.

After the Revolution, life in the Cossack villages of southern Russia changed, but not as dramatically as in less isolated spots. Bred on freedom, the people treasured their past and resisted innovation. The one institution that changed them, that homogenized them, that lifted them inexorably into the modern age was the schools. Like Raisa, Mikhail excelled in school, and as it was for her, education was his chief means of social and economic ascent. However many ways that the Soviet Union and the United States are different, they share one ideal: the sons of ordinary farmers and laborers in both countries can become the American president or the Kremlin chief, although daughters are, in most cases, likely only to become their wives.

A final note to the Gorbachevs' pre-college careers: upon her high school graduation, Raisa was among that select minority—one in a hundred students—who received the coveted gold medal; Mikhail was among a less select minority and received only a silver one.

 *TWO*

Student Days

A GROUP PHOTOGRAPH taken in 1954 at the end of the academic year consists of 132 portraits: twenty-two staff members and 110 students in the philosophy faculty (department) of Moscow State University. On the bottom row, fourth from the left, is a serious-looking young woman staring intently into the camera. The picture is labeled "Titorenko, R. M.," but that was no longer her name.

Having married her fellow student Mikhail the previous year, she was now Raisa Gorbachev. "Titorenko" appears for two reasons. First, most of her classmates knew her by that name and, second, due to restrictions on social and sexual life under Stalin, student marriages were frequently short-lived. The rules, insofar as they could be enforced, allowed sexual intercourse only between married couples—and they were enforced not by security guards, but by circumstances. The dormitories were so crowded that it was barely possible to study, let alone make love. Consequently, to escape the puritanical and cloistered environment of the hostels, students frequently married in haste. The result: an extremely high divorce rate and a great many short-lived last names. Thus, it made more sense for women students to go by their original names.

The photograph is interesting—useful, anyway—for other reasons. Except for it, there is little consistent proof of the dates when Raisa started and finished school. It may be a careless omission or a deliberate one (even Russian First Ladies, perhaps, like to appear younger), but the photograph seems to establish beyond any doubt the hardly controversial fact that Raisa entered the university in 1949 and was graduated in 1954.

For equally perplexing reasons, the photograph was hard to obtain. Every time I tried, it would vanish immediately from whatever spot a beleaguered biographer could logically expect to find it. This seemed strange, not to mention irritating, until finally a clue emerged: when her husband was made Kremlin boss, Raisa apparently demanded the return of all photographs and personal documents. There are, therefore, very few photographs of her and even less information except what she or the party wishes to divulge. As a result, there is all sorts of confusion, even concerning as innocent a fact as when Raisa went to school.

All students, at least in theory, had a chance for a university education. One of the first articles of the constitution of the new government under Lenin insured the right to universal free education. But under Stalin the state did not carry through with this promise, at least in the same egalitarian spirit of the original pledge. The gold medal Raisa received when she graduated from high school assured her of a place at a university. Which university (and the quality varied) depended on other factors: proximity (students were encouraged to study close to home) and political "pull" (in Russian, *blat*).

Blat, of course, refers to connections. Members of the

nomenklatura—top officials or people who had parents
or grandparents whose political loyalty as "Old Guard"
revolutionaries gave them *blat* for life—were able to
bypass the rules. Medals and distinctions helped, relatives high up in the party bureaucracy even more. As the
daughter of a railway worker, Raisa had none of these
advantages. Her only assets were earned, though they
were considerable: she had distinguished herself at
school and by her contributions to the Young Communist League (Komsomol), a youth organization and
training ground for party cadres. Her extreme shyness
was noted, possibly as a handicap, but her social commitment was felt to be so intense that the authorities
judged her worthy of a place at the leading Soviet university, Moscow State. And this, despite the considerable handicap of having had to constantly switch schools
and please an ever-changing constellation of teachers,
administrators, and officials. That she did was further
proof of her ambition and a certain kind of skill: to play
by the rules and come out on top.

IT IS POSSIBLE that during a balmy evening
in late summer of 1949, a young girl with braided hair
stood in the Byelorussian Station in Moscow. Her suitcase, much too heavy for her, probably contained everything she owned: her favorite books and her entire
wardrobe of summer and winter clothes—some dresses
and sweaters, a coat, a few skirts.

She was tired from her journey—from the Urals,
where Raisa had spent her last year at school, to Moscow was more than 60 miles—but that was hardly in-
timidating for a Russian, certainly not for a Russian
railroad worker's daughter. Besides, she had other
things on her mind: home, her parents, the excitement
of finally arriving in Moscow, and the future: what hers
might be like.

Now, though, she was probably overwhelmed. The

scene at the station was typical mayhem: thousands of weary travelers pressing toward the exit; others, standing beside mounds of luggage, waiting for a train whose departure had been announced for that day but not yet at any particular time. "When will the train come? When will the train come?" people ask. *"Budyet, budyet,"* the railway men counsel. "Patience, patience, it will be here soon."

Clinging to her cardboard box and suitcase (for even a pair of shoes was hard to replace, let alone an entire wardrobe), Raisa walked to the front of the station to an even more chaotic scene: small armies of people being picked up or dropped off by open-topped trunks; others trying to jump on the running-boards of an already overloaded bus. Rural Russia simply spews people into the capital; it's where everyone wants to be.

Though Raisa had probably never been to Moscow, even a young girl from Vessolayarsk would undoubtedly have seen pictures of Red Square, the Metro, the Kremlin where the window of the great and wise Comrade Stalin was lit day and night. But from outside the train station, its glories were still under a pall, after the rigors of the war years. And everywhere, it seemed, were disabled men and women—victims of that brutal conflagration.

Moscow was always exciting—home of the famous GUM department store, Lenin's Tomb, the archives where so much post-Revolutionary knowledge was stored—and full of energy, its aggressive individuality both captivating and grating. But it was even more energetic and exciting during the era in which Raisa arrived. After the war, the revitalization of Moscow had been given top priority by the Kremlin. Food supplies, always more plentiful than in other parts of Russia, were even more abundant now with the surge of postwar funds. In downtown Moscow, there was food for sale that Raisa had probably never even seen before: caviar, prawns, smoked fish. But the prices were so high that, like most of the city's population, students could only press their noses against the windows. It was a familiar student invitation in those days: "Let's go into the city and feast our eyes."

Raisa's destination was Stromynka Street in Sokolniki, the district in northeast Moscow where most of the student hostels were. Raisa's hostel had particular historical significance—it was the old army barracks used by the Preobrazhensky Cavalry Regiment during the reign of Peter the Great in the seventeenth century. But what it lacked in charm, it made up for in history. After the Revolution of 1917, an additional story was added to the buildings, but that was probably the last renovation in this century. However dilapidated, it was deemed adequate for students.

Conditions inside were strictly primitive. More than ten thousand people lived in the converted barracks, seven to fifteen in a room. Men and women stayed on different floors, and regulations were strict. Romantically inclined students had to use considerable ingenuity, which they managed via coded door knocks and cleaning schedules calculated to give the lovers at least a few minutes alone. Not only did supervisors have to be outwitted, roommates had to be persuaded to billet themselves elsewhere at appropriate times.

On each floor was a communal lavatory, a washbasin, and rudimentary cooking facilities. Anyone in search of better hygiene could go to the public baths, but that required more rubles than most students could afford. Each student had a bed but not necessarily his or her own chair, and instead of pictures of relatives or friends on the walls, it was Lenin whose piercing eyes gazed down upon them.

Raisa's room accommodated twelve. Judged by the standards of a real army barracks, it was luxurious: twelve beds, a few bedside tables, even a wardrobe. But the wardrobe was so small that the students had to keep most of their possessions in suitcases and boxes under their beds. The room had a table but not enough chairs for everyone to sit down at once. The windows were adorned by neither curtain nor shade. In winter, the bare panes let in too much cold; in summer, too much sun, making the cramped space suffocatingly hot.

"We lived in Room 392. Twelve women students lived there together. We were a bit short of space, as you can imagine," Ida Ivanovna Schulz, a student with Raisa and now a professor of party history at the Technical Institute in Vladimir, east of Moscow, recalled. "The floor was bare concrete without floorboards or, of course, a carpet. When we scrubbed the floor, it took three days to dry. We took turns doing the cleaning. Although living conditions were terribly cramped, we got along together very happily. At the end of the first academic year, there were seven of us in the room, then six, and eventually four—Raisa, Nina Mordasova, Khalida Siyatdinova, and myself. At midday we ate in the school canteen. We weren't too fussy about food; all we wanted was a hot meal. Whoever could guess the main ingredient was regarded as a culinary genius (usually the dish was a pottage based on buckwheat or millet). In the evening we made a casserole of potatoes for everybody. Raisa's parents sent us food parcels. I remember that Raisa and Khalida were sent honey quite often. Anything we received, we shared between us. We were never actually hungry. Our average grant was about thirty rubles. That was not very much, and many parents helped out with food parcels or a few extra rubles. Dunechka, one of our fellow students, had no one to support her. So each of us used to put a little money aside regularly to see her through. There were no problems of nationality. We all lived together very contentedly, a girl from Armenia, one from Azerbaijan, another from Uzbekistan."

The wealth of different backgrounds added another element to the students' education. Students converged at Moscow State from all over the map: every province in the Soviet Union as well as satellite countries in the Eastern bloc. A few students even came from the West, sent by their national Communist parties to study in the capital city of the "true doctrine." All the students in Raisa's dormitory were studying in one of the two branches of the philosophy faculty: philosophy, like Raisa's friend Ida, or psychology, which is what Raisa chose.

In her dormitory as in others, poverty gave rise to solidarity, which in turn gave rise to certain practical rules. Barely able to live on their meager student grants, they scrimped and saved collectively. They took turns shopping and cooking the potato casserole for the evening meal, sometimes supplemented with curd cheese or herring.

Both the school day and school week were long. Classes began at 8:00 A.M. and ended at 5:00 P.M. every day but Sunday. From the barracks it was a quick walk to the Metro, then an hour's trip to the university. Fortunately, the philosophy building was only a few steps from the library, which, given the overcrowded conditions of the hostels, was a much more pleasant place to work, with its huge, circular marble halls. Few students had to be pressed to work. They viewed studying not only as a responsibility but as an honor. And for those who didn't, there were rules: attendance at lectures was compulsory, and absences were punished by disciplinary measures ranging from threats to withdraw a student's grant to final expulsion.

As a student's sole means of support, grants were essential. The amount of the stipend hinged largely on academic work—luckily for Raisa. "From the beginning, Raisa received a bigger grant than the rest of us, a reward for the gold medal she had won in Krasnodar for

her brilliant school results," her friend Ida Schulz recalled. "But she did not rest on her laurels; she was
extremely single-minded about her studies. We were all
young then, just eighteen, but not children. We knew it
was our duty to study, and we did that wholeheartedly."

And not under the most comfortable conditions. "It
really was impossible to work in our room at the hostel,
twelve girls in such a tiny space. We only went back
there to sleep. We prepared for our seminars in the reading room at the university library on Machovaya Street.
To make sure of a place, you had to get up very early
and be outside the library when the reading room
opened at seven o'clock. I often kept a place for Raisa,
and sometimes she did the same for me. None of us was
lazy, but Raisa was a bit more conscientious than anybody else. We were all children of working-class parents
who had themselves received only a rudimentary education. We wanted to be better educated than they were,
to make use of the opportunity we had been given. We
arrived from all corners of the USSR, filled with an ambition to conquer the capital."

Studying, too, Ida Schulz remarked, was often a cooperative endeavor. "We used to prepare for our seminars together. A student well versed in a particular
subject would test the others in it. Even a few ex-soldiers
and officers of the Red Army who had served at the
front were members of our study group. They had been
demobilized and were equipping themselves for civilian
life. They were, of course, older than us and inclined to
be patronizing."

Stalin died in 1953, in Raisa's fourth year at the university. All classes were suspended. For two days, Raisa
and her roommates stood in Soyuzov Hall (the Hall of
the Trade Unions), where Stalin's body lay on a bier.
Raisa caught a bad cold, Schulz recalled, but otherwise
her reaction to Stalin's death was typical: she wept.

How the daughter of Maxim Titorenko could weep

for her father's oppressor was a question that might have been asked not only of Raisa but of many Russians. But it was a question one could only begin to answer by looking at Russia's past. They were a people who for centuries had known little other than autocratic rule, so their relationship to Stalin was not so unique. Some political theorists have likened the appeal of a charismatic leader, even a brutal one, to that of an abusive parent: the child may fear and hate the parent, but also need him, depend on him, revere him, and in some strange, mortal way, even love him. And then there were the repressive tactics of the police state to make sure that whatever the people felt, at least they obeyed. During his roughly thirty-year reign, Stalin had thousands of enemies but, as evidenced by the massive outpouring of grief at his death, he left many more fans, among them Raisa Maximovna Titorenko.

LIFE FOR Soviet students was not all politics and work. Nearly all of them had arrived in Moscow from the provinces, and the lure of city life was great. Even during times of scarcity, Moscow provided one type of nourishment that made its inhabitants forget their hunger: culture. Raisa ventured out into this exciting world, and quickly came under the spell of music, art, and theater. It was an attraction that would last throughout her life. In this sense, she was Maxim Titorenko's daughter, but what he had only talked about with Likhachev, she could now experience firsthand.

Students tumbled out of the theaters and museums, arguing heatedly about art, literature, and life. Books were the focus of passionate discussion, with everyone borrowing and lending them, sometimes furtively if the book had a whiff of dissidence about it. Evoking the richness of those days, Ida Schulz recalls that "in Moscow we had our first experience of opera, and we saw performances of the highest standard the Soviet Union could then offer. What did we see? The answer is simple. Raisa and I saw pretty well the entire repertoire of the Bolshoi. We heard the most renowned singers in the USSR; we saw the most brilliant ballet dancers. Ulanova, the famous ballerina, was dancing at the Bolshoi; her Dying Swan was known throughout the world. We went to the Moscow theaters, where we saw the most stunning productions. Through the University Club, we took out subscriptions for all of Moscow's principal cultural events. The crowds were enormous. Trying to get into an event the normal way, through a box-office booking, was almost impossible, the demand was so great. We did manage somehow to get in once or twice a week to a play, an opera, or a concert. Dancing was very popular, especially the tango. I always remember the old tango 'Jealousie,' one of our favorites."

Into this full and exciting life, Raisa packed other events. At dances organized by the Komsomol, the shy girl from the Altai Mountains with the thick, reddish braids cast off her shyness and joined in the fun. At a student theater club too, there was a spontaneous outpouring of energy, enthusiasm, and ideas. Like many of her classmates, the first postwar generation of Soviet youth, she was eager to enjoy life, to make up for what her generation and that of her parents had missed during the war.

"Oh, yes, we had a good time," Ida Schulz recalled. "I can still remember the New Year's Eve party we had in our first year," she said, pointing to a photograph of a group of students. "We took all the beds out of our room and pushed the table into the middle. Raisa Maximovna was wearing a white dress that day. The man in the front wearing boots is Vitya Gorliansky, who is now professor of philosophy at the Conservatory in Gorky. Next to Raisa is Lydia Rusinova, wife of a well-known philosopher, Yuri Levanda. There he is, sitting in the front row on the extreme right. Lydia was working in

Smolensk, until she died in a car crash. Here you can see other friends of Raisa's, Ida Solovieva and the skinny little Hungarian, Leila Grigorian. In the second row, looking from left to right, Slava Kalinen, who is now on the staff of an important new agency, APN; Leonid Che-potarev, who died of cancer; Chamrakol Meltykpotarev from Uzbekistan, a university lecturer. He was ten years older than the rest of us and had been chairman of a collective farm for several years before he became a student. That one there, he was a real Count Vronsky. We called him 'the Comet.' He suddenly appeared on our horizon and disappeared just as quickly. Nina Morda-sova and Mirab Mirabmarmadashvili were also part of our group, but they are not in the photograph.

"We all got along together easily, as you can imagine," Schulz went on. "New Year's Eve was a good excuse for having a meal together, relaxing, having a chat. There were no tensions between us. I remember Raisa that evening in her long white dress, with her slender waist, high heels, and hair braided around her head. She had no lack of admirers. Although the women philosophy students were all clever and attractive, the men seemed to prefer the psychology students. Why? I don't know. Perhaps the psychology students didn't talk so much."

In Moscow, the country girl began to acquire a veneer of sophistication. First came a more cosmopolitan hair-style. "In the first year Raisa wore her hair in long plaits, braided around her head. Then she had it cut off and let it wave naturally," Schulz recalled. Then came a marked interest in clothes. "In 1951, she and Nina Mordasova ordered dark blue coats from a tailor's shop not far from the Preobrazhensky hostel. Raisa's coat had a little collar of Persian lamb." That bit of luxury was thanks to her larger student grant. "Raisa was always very con-cerned about her friend Nina, who had lived in an or-phanage before she came to the university," Schulz said.

"Her only relative, an aunt, worked in the Soviet Embassy in America and could not give her niece financial support until she returned to the USSR. I myself had to wait a year longer before I could afford a tailor-made coat. Until then, I had to make do with a coat belonging to my mother, which I had worn ever since I arrived in Moscow in 1949."

The new Raisa, however, did not forget the old, nor her relatives, nor her roots. "Raisa was very fond of her brother and sister, Genya [Evgeny] and Lyudoshka [Ludmilla], who were several years younger," Schulz recalled. "Lyudoshka later studied psychology at Moscow State University, while Genya became a cadet at a military academy." As for Raisa's parents, they visited her only once, but that was more than many students' families could afford. According to Schulz, it was an unusually pleasant experience, with Raisa's parents becoming, for a weekend, parents to them all. "They slept in the same room as their daughter in the hostel in Stromynka Street, the other students willingly making room for them. All of Raisa's friends cooked meals for her parents. All one big family. Most of the students hardly ever saw their own parents, so they were grateful to be able to talk over their problems with surrogate parents. The atmosphere was cozy; Raisa's father was especially sociable. Her mother sewed on buttons and did some mending for the other girls. Who would have guessed, then, that one day there would be so much interest in Raisa and her life?"

Raisa's life as a student continued with its mix of scholarship, social life, and cultural activities. And then there were her more trivial pleasures, ranging from clothes-swapping to aerobics à la USSR. "We used to swap clothes regularly," Schulz recalled. "When one girl had a date, the others would offer her their best dresses. A date being something of an occasion, you needed to look your best. Don't forget, the boys had quite a lot of choice.

"Raisa was always ready to try something new in her limited spare time. She and Nina Mordasova took a class in rhythmic gymnastics, which was trendy at the time. Nina had a problem with her weight. Unfortunately, she got even fatter and had to give the gymnastics up. Raisa carried on with it, as far as I can remember. In her relationships with other students, Raisa usually took the leading role. She was quickwitted and had fast reactions."

Beginning in 1953, the students moved into the new university building in the Lenin Hills. "I think we were actually the first students there," Schulz recalled. "We loaded our belongings onto trucks and drove merrily through the whole city. A new university and a new hostel, it was like heaven. There were even tablecloths and waiters in the dining hall. While the new university was under construction, all the students from the philosophy faculty were active as party propagandists. Once a week, we spoke to the workers—they had all been released from labor camps not long before—and through discussion tried to educate them politically. Most of the workers, though, were not too keen to talk to us. And when they did tell us something about life in the camps, we quite simply didn't believe them. Quite a few of us thought, in fact, that people who said such bad things about the government belonged in a camp anyway." If Raisa took part in these student-run lectures, Schulz doesn't say.

"What else can I tell you about Raisa? I think I've told you everything already," her friend concluded. "She was open, she liked to sing, she was always humming some tune or other. I remember her as a radiant young woman, full of life, always good-tempered."

Another of Raisa's fellow students, Valentin Sidorov, now an esteemed writer on Indian philosophy, found Raisa not only a stimulating friend but a generous one. Once, his mother came to visit unexpectedly. There were no hotel rooms in Moscow and, of course, she wasn't permitted to stay in his room. He was explaining to her that she would have to travel home that same night when Raisa intervened and, without any fuss, gave up her own bed, moving into another room so that Sidorov's mother could stay.

Among the brightest students and with consistently excellent grades, Raisa received an achievement bonus each month in addition to her grant, which, because of her gold medal, was already high. Financially, therefore, she was better off than most of her colleagues (hence, the fur-collared coat). Yet she was not immune to their plight. Sidorov, with whom she shared a love of classical music and Dostoevsky, was unable to live off his grant and frequently borrowed money from her at the end of the month.

Among his most lingering memories is the night in June 1954 when they all received their diplomas. Happy and relaxed, they wandered through the streets of Moscow, each holding a candle. For many in the group, it would be their last meeting with Raisa. There were annual student reunions at the Moskva or the National Hotel in subsequent years, but Raisa never went. Perhaps it was too long a journey or perhaps she was too immersed in the present to take time out for the past, even such an exciting one.

She did see Sidorov again. In 1986 she accompanied her husband to a writers' congress in Moscow. She at once recognized her former classmate, and began to talk animatedly about old times. "We talked just as easily as we used to when we were students—though now I don't have to touch her for the odd ruble," he recalled with a smile. Although it had been thirty-two years, Raisa, with her interest in literature, had faithfully followed her friend's career. She paid him the highest compliment a writer could wish: she not only owned his books, she had read them.

For all the exuberance of student life, the same sinister cloud that hung over the rest of Soviet life darkened the academic world. The utmost circumspection was required in one's choice of intellectual passions. Any professor who departed from official orthodoxy was subject to expulsion or worse—summary execution or a slow death in a gulag. The rigid Marxist dogma under Stalin had an especially destructive effect on philosophy, Raisa's field (psychology and sociology, her majors, were subsections). The discipline was now reduced to one crude formula: the struggle between materialism and idealism. Materialism was viewed as progressive and forward-looking, idealism as retrograde and reactionary. Marx, Lenin, Engels, and Stalin, leaders in political theory, were also regarded as the greatest philosophers (not to mention historians, linguists . . .), whereas the works of Western philosophers such as Kant and Hegel were banned.

Among the leading textbooks of "the science of knowledge," as this new field was dubbed, were two by Lenin, *Marxism and the Study of Language* and *The Economic Problems of Socialism in the USSR*. The result was that entire areas of social science were dismantled or distorted. But course content wasn't the only victim of Stalin's educational ideas. The faculty was affected, too. Alongside professors of outstanding intellectual ability droned ignorant amateurs. The role of guardian of "intellectual Communism" in the philosophy faculty, for example, was assumed by a man whose previous job was as a warden in a prison camp for juvenile delinquents.

Fields other than philosophy suffered as well. In biology, the classical theory of genetics was demolished as a bourgeois half-truth and its exponents denounced as charlatans or, worse, "bourgeois" thinkers. In its place and elevated to the status of science were the genetic theories of a poorly educated agronomist, Trofim Lysenko, whom Stalin admired. Anyone who objected forfeited his university job, with the sad result that many scientists who had earlier known international acclaim found it hard to get work even as street sweepers. Some suffered physical and mental abuse as well.

Obviously, no student could remain immune. In lectures and seminars, every philosophical problem was refracted through the prism of Stalinism; everything was related to the class struggle, to Marxist dialectical materialism, to the Communist Party. Professors preached a version of Stalinism that was given such a powerful philosophical gloss that students accepted it as the preeminent wisdom of their time. Raisa, like her colleagues, expressed enthusiasm for Stalin's genius and believed implicitly in the imminent victory of Communism. She made liberal use of quotations from famous Communist writers in her work, which obviously pleased her professors: she earned a continuous run of good grades and favorable reports.

Among the other students with whom Raisa was friendly were Nikolai Lapin and Nail Bikkenin. Both were hardworking and conscientiously conformed to party discipline. When she completed her studies, she let many friendships lapse, but not her friendship with these two men, which hardly hurt their careers. At least for a brief period, Lapin's career seemed to prosper from his association with Raisa. After graduation from Moscow State, he became scientific editor of the academic journal *Voprosy Filosofii (Problems of Philosophy)*, put out by the philosophy faculty. He later transferred to the Philosophy Institute of the Academy of Science, but after clashing with the director was, for many years, banished to a third-rate school. Only with Gorbachev's ascension did Lapin's prospects improve. With scarcely a published article to his name, he suddenly became deputy director and then director of the Philosophy Institute of the Academy of Sciences. His resurrection, however, was short-lived. Gorbachev soon replaced him with Ivan Frolov, his adviser on culture and science and, since 1989, the editor in chief of *Pravda*.

Bikkenin's success was more lasting. After working with Lapin on the philosophy journal, he moved to the ideology section of the Central Committee of the Communist Party. There, his principal task was to counter the influence of Western thought and attitudes in the USSR. Since Gorbachev's rise, Bikkenin has been in charge of *The Communist,* the party's ideological weekly. It is difficult to explain what Gorbachev, a reformer, hoped to achieve by entrusting this important position to someone as cautious and conservative as Bikkenin. The grapevine points to Raisa.

Another of Raisa's contemporaries followed a much different route. Alexander Zinoviev became an outspoken critic of the Communist Party. His popular *Yawning Heights,* a satirical novel, lampoons the party for mismanagement and abuse of privilege. Supporters of *perestroika* are lambasted, too, including Gorbachev's hand-picked successor to Lapin, Ivan Frolov. Not surprisingly, even under *glasnost,* where almost no subject is taboo in the Soviet press, Zinoviev's book remains banned.

THERE IS a faded old photograph that shows Raisa and her roommates sitting on Raisa's bed. It is quite a cosmopolitan group, though different from the original set of roommates—Khalida Siyatdinova, now a professor of philosophy at a college in Tashkent, joined them in 1952, Raisa's third year at the university—and yet, somehow, Raisa stands out. Whether through some small gesture, the tilt of her head, her clothes—in this case, a dark, printed dress—it is Raisa to whom the viewer is drawn. And this remains true in later photographs, especially those with other Soviet leaders' wives. Look at the portrait of Raisa and the wife of Premier Nikolai Ryzhkov. Mrs. Ryzhkov is wearing a brightly colored scarf, and yet one's eye turns quickly to Raisa. Perhaps it's her confidence, her clothes—unlike Mrs. Ryzhkov's, obviously tailor-made—or maybe her dark, intelligent eyes. Whatever the elusive quality, it is possibly what attracted her two serious suitors during her university years.

Oleg, slim, good-looking, a general's son, was the first man undeterred by Raisa's reserve, and he pursued her ardently during her undergraduate years. A favorite activity of young couples was to walk through the Moscow parks, and there, wandering among the birch trees or sitting on one of the ornate white benches, Oleg and Raisa spent many hours. Evidently he was serious enough to bring her home to his mother. The meeting, however, was a disaster. Having found out about Raisa's lineage—that she was the daughter of an ordinary railway worker—Oleg's mother declared her unsuitable. A dutiful son, Oleg obeyed. There were no more walks in the park.

Her next suitor was of more appropriately humble origins. They met at a student dancing class in 1951. Raisa went because she loved to dance, but Mikhail, studying law at the time, went to accompany (and poke fun at) a friend. Like Raisa, he was good-looking and confident, but as for other qualities, they had yet to be discerned. When Raisa injured her foot in a gymnastics class and had to go to the hospital, Mikhail, who had not forgotten their first meeting, went to visit her. Evidently he was quite a hit, at least with the nurses. "He's a real heart-throb," one said. "Don't let him get away."

"They were very much in love, very happy together," Ida Schulz recalled. "In my opinion, they complemented each other ideally. I doubt whether Mikhail Gorbachev would have achieved as much as he has if he had married somebody else. When Raisa got to know Mikhail, she was rather uncertain in her attitude toward men. She

had just experienced a somewhat disillusioning love affair. She often asked Nina Mordasova for advice."

Mikhail might have been a shy boy from the country,
but he was not inexperienced. At the time, he was seeing
a girl named Svetlana Koryashkina. It was only after he
met Raisa that he ended his relationship with her. (According to the Moscow grapevine, Raisa still gets quite
annoyed if anyone teases her about Svetlana.)

"It was a case of love at first sight for Mikhail Gorbachev, but not for Raisa," Schulz recalls. "He had to
court her patiently for a year before she would say yes.
Over that year, he gave her reassurance, being an intelligent man who inspired confidence. He was strong-
willed, impressively serious-minded, an outstanding
student. He fitted into our circle easily. We liked him.
We could see from the beginning what his intentions
were regarding Raisa. It's good when a young man be-
haves like that, isn't it?"

Their courtship took place at dances, concerts, and
plays. The cultural backdrop was largely owing to Raisa,
who, friends say, awakened a similar interest in Mikhail.
They took part in student theatricals; he read her poetry
in the park. In the evenings, they wandered through
Moscow. During these walks, Mikhail carried the
lighted candle that students used as a symbol of their
love. They wanted to get married, but Raisa's parents
objected. They felt that both should finish their studies
first. Raisa and Mikhail, in this case, did not toe the
party line.

Their wedding, in 1953 (Raisa was twenty-one,
Mikhail twenty-three), was a happy affair, done in the
usual bare-bones but high-spirited Komsomol style. After the legal ceremony at the city registry office, there
was a breakfast for some thirty fellow students in the
school dining hall, and, for once, they did not have to
drink the infamous student tea ("brown water"); someone had gotten hold of a samovar and brewed proper

Russian tea. And from the bridegroom's mother, sausage and salted meat from Privolnoye. (Neither his parents nor hers attended the wedding; this was strictly a student affair.) After the party, Mikhail and Raisa set off for their fabulous honeymoon: one night in Mikhail's room minus his roommates.

The next day they were back at school, and the next night and every night in the months to come, back to separate rooms on separate floors. Only a year later were they able to move into a room together. In the meantime, Mikhail found various ways to circumvent their problem, most of which involved his roommates taking sudden "trips."

The newlyweds continued their busy life, sometimes together and sometimes alone. Much of Mikhail's time was devoted to what was called "community work": campaigns, meetings, and discussions in the Komsomol about the future of Communism, now that Stalin was dead. He soon became a student representative on the Komsomol's faculty management committee. (As such, he was criticized in a newspaper article by another official, Anatoly Lukyanov. Apparently Gorbachev isn't one to hold a grudge: Lukyanov is currently his number two man in the Congress of the People's Deputies.)

Together, Raisa and her husband tended to participate more in cultural events, and could often be found at the cinema, the Bolshoi and, on weekends, at the open-air concerts in Luzhniki Park, with its typical Soviet mix of dance, song and orchestral music. If at first Mikhail went mainly to please his wife, eventually he seemed to appreciate the programs himself.

In 1954, Stromynka Street and all its discomforts were left behind. Mikhail and Raisa moved into the new hostel in the Lenin Hills, which by comparison seemed like a first-class hotel. The short time that they spent there before leaving Moscow was the happiest of their student years. Reflecting back on that time in the Lenin Hills,

Gorbachev later said, "It was unique. Without that experience, I don't think my life would have turned out as it has."

The years immediately following the death of Stalin were difficult years for the Soviet Union. The country underwent a period of paralysis, with all political initiative frozen. It took time for the country to awaken from its deep sleep, and it was during that period of awakening that the Gorbachevs spent their final years at school. For some, it was a time of grief. Many citizens wept at the grave of the dictator. They did not believe, or did not want to believe, the rumors about him starting to emerge. And yet they obviously felt a desire for a different way of life. The poetry of the young Yevgeny Yevtushenko expressed the hopes of contemporary young Russians: to live, to work, to love—in freedom.

Raisa finished her studies a year ahead of Mikhail. In her finals, she was awarded exceptionally high grades and was immediately offered a research fellowship, which meant going on for her doctorate. Raisa accepted, partly because she was eager to continue her studies and partly in hope that she and Mikhail could remain in Moscow. But neither goal proved possible. As soon as Mikhail completed his studies, he was ordered to Stavropol. For Raisa, this meant an end to their happy life in Moscow and postponing, at least for now, further scholarly work. As the Soviet saying goes, "The comrade reflects, the party directs."

 *THREE*

Stavropol

IN 1955 IN SOVIET RUSSIA, new entrants to any profession were not given a great deal of latitude in choosing where to go. University graduates, having enjoyed the special privilege of a higher education, had to serve three years in whatever cadres the Soviet government assigned them. The principle was simple: the state paid for the student's education, accommodations, and a grant on which to live, in return, the student had a moral debt to the state. In fact, at the beginning of his university career, each student had to sign a pledge to go wherever the state decreed. Only students who achieved brilliant results or demonstrated "exemplary behavior"—unquestioning subservience to the party—could hope to have the slightest say in their posting. The Gorbachevs might have had such a say and requested to stay in Moscow, but Mikhail had other ideas. The alternative, Stavropol, the largest city in the region where he grew up, had one key advantage over Moscow: he could become a big fish in a small pond.

Certainly, the decision was not easy given Raisa's attachment to Moscow. After years in that exciting capital, she would be hard pressed to find intellectual stimulation in the culturally stagnant environment of the provinces. No more metropolitan pleasures, no more evenings at the Bolshoi, and in exchange for city chic, the dull rhythm of rural life. She might as well have gone back to Vessolayarsk. Nonetheless, she yielded, though "yielded" may be too strong a word. She was a woman and a scholar, but she was also a product of the 1950s, and her husband's career came first. Had she considered giving priority to her own career, she would have been an even more unusual woman than she was.

They quickly packed their few possessions and boarded a train to Stavropol, capital of the region of the same name on the northern edge of the Caucasus, but considerably inland from the Black Sea. Their arrival could hardly have been less auspicious. The room they were allocated was little more than a closet, with no bathroom. Even compared to their student quarters, it looked grim. Their only consolation was the countryside. The area around Stavropol was luxuriant, and the climate blessedly mild. Winter, endless in Moscow, here lasted only three months, and then there was April. Raisa had never experienced anything like it: the warm breeze, the purple sky, foliage everywhere. Nature made up for some of the things she missed about Moscow, but not all.

Stavropol, with its population of barely 100,000, was somewhere between a city and a town. The downtown area was occupied by multistory brick buildings, but once you left its perimeters the atmosphere suddenly changed. Here there were expanses of green fields and modest houses with gardens in which families grew their own food. Most of the families were of peasant stock and retained some pre-Revolutionary ideas, one of which was profit. If they happened to have a surplus crop, they simply went to the market and sold it. The market served not only as a commercial center but as a social one: you went to hear local news, gossip, and what little news about the outside world that made its way down here.

One feature distinguished Stavropol from an ordinary rural province. A cluster of natural springs, whose waters are said to have curative powers, lay at the heart of the region, and around them, a number of well-known spas. Even in the time of the tsars, places like Mineralniye Vody, Pyatigorsk, and Kislovodsk had reputations as excellent health resorts. Today, Kremlin leaders, party bosses, generals, and other members of the elite come to the region with their wives and children to "take the waters" or recuperate in any of numerous spas: about eighty sanatoriums and twenty hotels that offer hydrotherapy, mud pack therapy, even cures for alcoholism (the Soviet national disease). Access to the best facilities, of course, is limited. In Kislovodsk, for example, only the higher ranks of army officials can use the sanatoriums, surrounded by dachas of the KGB.

Even more beneficial than the waters, were those who "took" them, and the opportunity this would provide Gorbachev in his climb up the party ranks. Eventually, as party chief of Stavropol, he would be responsible for welcoming these visitors and showing them around, no small task considering they often spent their entire vacations in Stavropol. The Gorbachevs thus had a vital opportunity to mingle with Moscow officials and their wives. As wife of the local first secretary, Raisa accompanied her husband on these excursions, and the impression she made on their visitors was striking.

This was especially true of Yuri Andropov, the KGB chief under Brezhnev. The normally aloof Andropov took note not only of Gorbachev's impressive qualities but also those of his wife. Raisa represented an entirely different woman from the usual run of provincial officials' wives. Well educated, she had her own interests and career, and yet she was intensely involved with her husband's career as well. In fact, they were mates. Except for Lenin and his wife, Krupskaya, you could not say that about many couples in Soviet lore.

But advancement did not come quite so quickly for the Gorbachevs. Long before they escorted any party chiefs around, they had their own humble tasks to fulfill. Gorbachev's first job in Stavropol was as deputy head of the propaganda department of the local Komsomol. Raisa obtained an unglamorous post as a tutor in philosophy at the Stavropol Agricultural Institute. Here, she did not even give lectures but led seminars, the lowest rung on the academic ladder.

But no matter how meager the position, Raisa was, by temperament, addicted to her job. "As long as I can remember she has talked incessantly about her work, what she has to do, how she must prepare for a lecture, which books she must read, how busy she is," her friend Lydia Budyka recalled. And though it was difficult work, the job was not unrewarding or irrelevant to the Gorbachevs' life. "As a result of her preparations for the seminars and her subsequent position as a lecturer, she accumulated mountains of books at home for study," Budyka said. The books broadened her knowledge and, through their sharing, her husband's as well.

In Stavropol, with its rich southern soil and abundant crops, the Gorbachevs had an ample quantity of fresh fruit, vegetables, and everything else. Sheep farmers from the foothills of Caucasus and farming families from the old Cossack villages supplied meat, milk, and cheese. For the first time in their married life, the Gorbachevs could indulge, but they did not. Even regarding food, Raisa took the practical view: she served fruits and vegetables daily and, unlike the typical Russian housewife, limited foods high in starches and fats.

After only a short while, Mikhail got his first promotion. He was now first secretary of the Stavropol Komsomol Committee, and as such a member, finally, of the nomenklatura, the political elite. Among the many perquisites he enjoyed was a staff car, which Raisa could use for shopping expeditions or trips into the country-side. But these luxuries—a car, fresh produce—were small compensation for the stimulating life left behind in Moscow, and it was a struggle for Raisa to adjust.

It was less of a struggle for Mikhail for two reasons. First, it was his career they were pursuing, and second, Stavropol was home. What was provincial to others was comfortably familiar, even charming, to him. Another factor was temperament. Mikhail wasn't as restless as his wife; he could be content with what he had. In fact, from Raisa's point of view, he was in danger of becoming too content. During most of their years in Stavropol, she battled against complacency. He must never be satisfied with his achievements, she argued. At the same time, she encouraged him to look beyond the narrow confines of politics, to scholarship and art. In both these ways, and a third—that she loved him—she was an ideal mate: an ambitious one who could stoke his fire and an intellectual one who could broaden his scope.

The staff car was only the beginning of their new, more privileged life. They now had a comfortable apartment and, as members of the nomenklatura, entrée into the best shops. Vacations, too, for the first time were possible. During their first few years in Stavropol, they had not been permitted to leave, adding to Raisa's sense of imprisonment. But now they could visit the most desirable spas and resorts all over the USSR.

But except for their trips to Moscow and occasional vacations, the Gorbachevs' lives were dominated by Mikhail's work. Every morning he disappeared into his office, where he remained until late at night, leaving only to visit one of the various youth organizations under his charge. In contrast, Raisa's life was considerably more idle. Aside from her job, she had only to manage the details of their domestic life. Her loneliness during this period was considerable, and it is not a time she likes to recall.

On January 6, 1958, their daughter, Irina Mikhailovna, was born. Raisa was a loving and devoted mother, but by no means overindulgent. Her friends still smile over an incident many years ago at a reception to celebrate International Women's Day, at which children were allowed. There were good things to eat on the table, and before the official speeches were even under way, little Irina had managed to steal away from her mother and was digging into the food. Raisa may have been horrified, but all she looked was cool. From across the hall, she called to Irina in a firm voice and instantly the child stopped. With a minimum of fuss, the other women noted, she had corrected the errant child, who now hid behind a curtain in retreat.

Alexander Herzen, the great nineteenth-century Russian democrat and philosopher, said that a woman who has borne a child truly serves the state, for becoming a mother is a woman's primary social function. A noble theory, but not one supported more than rhetorically by the state. For millions of Soviet women, motherhood was only a second career and, from economic necessity, not the one at which they spent the better part of their time. It was not only a question of money (and there was no paid maternity leave), but also of food coupons, which one could only get through a job. No work, no coupons: the "nobility" of motherhood came at a high price.

Thanks to their membership in the nomenklatura, Raisa was an exception to this rule. But the privileges she took for granted in Stavropol did not apply once she left. When in Moscow she, like any other housewife, had to stand in long lines at stores, and often came away empty-handed.

The birth of her daughter marked a change in Raisa's life. She seemed to become more social, accepting invitations from party cohorts to spend family holidays in the Caucasus Mountains or on the Black Sea. These trips, however, were rarely with friends of her choosing. The nomenklatura dictated whose company was acceptable, and usually it was their own.

Among her closest friends from that time was Lydia Budyka. A pediatrician, she treated Raisa's daughter, and her husband, as secretary of agriculture of the City Committee, was a colleague of Mikhail's. Budyka recalls the carefree quality of those days on the way up. "Life was freer, as it often is in the provinces, more open," she said. "Mikhail had his work for the Komsomol and also his party work, and there was a large circle of friends. We were all young and sociable and enjoyed being together. We celebrated all the main public holidays together, usually in a sizable group. We all used to meet at one another's houses and listen to music. We were all working, men and women, and we would go around after work to somebody's place and the women would make pilmeni [a kind of meat dumpling], sometimes the men too. It was an honest, open and happy life.

"On Sundays we would drive to Lake Seengileevskoye, about six miles from Stavropol, to relax. The men worked together during the week, but on weekends we all went out together, taking the children, and generally getting to know each other. We had a wonderful time."

Raisa's friendship with Lydia Budyka lasted beyond their Stavropol years. To this day, they remain the closest of friends. "As far as I'm concerned, she hasn't changed in the slightest," Budyka said. "I can still give her my opinion on a whole range of things, knowing she will listen to me, although whether we agree or not is another question." Naturally, they see each other less now. Budyka finds she has to phone several times before she is put through to Raisa, but the closeness endures. "We have a really good relationship, a genuine friendship," she said.

The trips into the countryside were among the more pleasant aspects of Stavropol life. For their Sunday excursions, the Gorbachevs and their friends would bring huge picnic baskets brimming with provisions. Activities would include a good ten- or fifteen-mile hike, after which they rewarded themselves with a hearty feast. Even the sternest party officials could look silly singing and taking photographs of themselves. For the more adventurous, there was climbing in the mountains. Some of the women, breathless because they were overweight, would be reluctant to continue, but Raisa would not give up until she reached the peak.

Photographs from that time show Raisa as the epitome of a certain type of Soviet woman: five foot two, sturdy, and with short but powerful legs. Her teeth look less even (perhaps she's had them capped), but her hair is as lovely as ever: a glowing reddish brown. Her face is plump, and her figure not so slender. Evidently, her weight was inversely proportional to her husband's position (the more he gained in stature, the more she lost in weight), or what she gained in sophistication, she lost in pounds.

Most of her spare time was spent with other nomenklatura wives, but not from choice. There were more intellectually compatible women to befriend in Stavropol—members of the agricultural, educational, and medical institutions—but most were beyond her reach. The strict rules of the nomenklatura allowed free association with members of these establishments only in exceptional cases. As a result, Raisa had to suffer through many an insipid luncheon and drink a great deal of unwanted tea.

Even beyond its tea parties, Stavropol was a stuffy place. Progressive ideas, especially in the arts, did not come quickly to Stavropol or to any regional area. The only compensation was the wide range of newspapers, periodicals, and books available, and those the Gorbachevs could not find locally, they had their friends send from Moscow. In that one sphere, their world was opening up. Khrushchev's denunciation of Stalin at the Twentieth Party Congress in 1956 brought a new spring to the Russian literary world. Books that had been banned for many years were now discussed freely. Histories were revised. The poems of Anna Akhmatova were published, as well as Solzhenitsyn's shocking exposé of the gulags. After years of physical and psychological terror, the effect was sensational: a blast of intellectual and spiritual energy was unleashed.

But not in Stavropol. The new books were available, but the clamor for them wasn't very great. Among the few who kept apace was Raisa, but for all her reading, who was there to share it with? Not her friends in the nomenklatura. But she did find an eager listener in her husband. A pattern was established early in their marriage: Raisa would give Mikhail a detailed summary of the books she had read, and then suggest which of them he ought to read himself. In this way, she had an outlet and was exposed to a wealth of powerful ideas.

Unfortunately, the higher Mikhail moved up the ladder, the less time they could spend together. But this was only one price of Gorbachev's admission to the nomenklatura. Some of the others were worse, at least for Raisa. Not only was she a resident of a small, provincial town, but she was forced to remain within a particularly conservative segment of it and obey its labyrinthine rules. Many of these rules, as comprehensive as Amy Vanderbilt's, regarded social life. Rule Number One: a wife should behave in a manner appropriate to her husband's rank within the hierarchy; i.e., the wife of the secretary of the City Komsomol Committee should defer to the wife of the secretary of the City Party Committee, because her husband's rank was higher. The free spirit who attempted to write her own rules would be ostracized by other wives or, worse, wreck her husband's career.

Rule Number Two: personal feelings were to be ignored in deciding whose invitations to accept; i.e., when the wife of a superior called, you went. This rule also worked in reverse. You couldn't say, "Let's go to the Petrovs'—they always have something interesting to dis-

cuss," if the Petrovs weren't among your acceptable social peers. Obviously, in such an environment, a person
had to be extremely well disciplined to survive.

And finally, Rule Number Three. The most important
rule, it assigned a woman her place and, most assuredly,
it was not at her husband's side. At the few official
events that women were allowed to attend, patriarchal
tradition (and here you couldn't blame the Bolsheviks)
dictated that a wife refrain from discussing her husband's work, airing her views about party affairs, and
participating in male conversation in general. In only
one respect were women considered equal. At official
receptions, there were usually endless speeches. Invariably, each speaker would propose a wordy toast, to
which the guests would respond by downing three
ounces of vodka—the women, too. This made the other
rules especially hard to obey. How to hold both your
liquor and your tongue?

In such an environment, Raisa naturally had to act the
part, which could not have been easy. (After one of the
Gorbachevs' visits to the United States, Senator Barbara
Mikulski of Maryland, referring to Raisa, quipped,
"This is the first person I've ever met who talks more
than I do." But that was many years later and a couple
of continents west.) In Stavropol, the rules brought forth
a different Raisa. The harmonious interchange that char-
acterized her private life with Mikhail was, in public,
forced underground along with the rest of her personality. It must have taken quite a bit of restraint to be a
nomenklatura wife, but then Raisa had nomenklatura
goals, and breaking the rules could have jeopardized her
husband's career.

Fortunately, Raisa had other outlets: her work, and
soon another project. After a few years in Stavropol, she
decided to begin work on her doctoral dissertation. Her
focus, dictated by conditions in Stavropol, now shifted
from psychology to sociology, which she had also stud-

ied in school. She took as her topic the economic and
social conditions of the collective farmer. The more research she did, the more aware of problems she became,
and with her practical, can-do attitude, of solutions,
too. From the beginning, she put her research at her
husband's service. Their home, as usual, became a fo-
rum for ideas. But now their roles became even more
tightly connected: she was studying firsthand the social
and economic conditions of his constituents. When he
left Stavropol, his greatest achievement was the increased agricultural output. If Raisa's work was helpful
to him, it was of greater value to her—the means by
which she kept her mind alive.

Despite its repressive side, there were aspects of
nomenklatura social life that would have been hard to
resist: the lavish hospitality, the abundance of superior
food and drink. A person didn't just invite you over for
a cup of tea, but for a splendid lunch and then an elaborate evening meal, with course after course, not to mention excellent wine (Stavropol had its own vineyards,
but the really good wine came from neighboring
Georgia).

And the goodies weren't limited to parties. Top officials had "arrangements" with the chairmen of collective farms and the Komsomol rural district committees
that ensured efficient supply lines between farms and the
tables of the local elite. Members of the leadership were
provided each month not only with regular deliveries of
meat, poultry, fruit, and vegetables, but also with sea-
sonal treats: in autumn, fish from the region's clear
streams; in winter, garlic sausages that, after the slaugh-
ter of the pigs, rural officials ordered specially prepared
(only the choicest meat for their influential friends).

Especially in the realm of food, the differences between nomenklatura and non-nomenklatura life were
startling. Even when poor harvests caused serious food
shortages for the locals, the larders of nomenklatura

families were well stocked. Naturally, the Gorbachevs shared in this bounty, their table richly spread not only for official entertaining but for national and private celebrations: May Day (May 1), Revolution Day (November 7), New Year's Day, family birthdays. Supplies from country to town suffered a continuing decline for many years, but a nomenklatura family was scarcely aware of this. Theirs truly was the Communist paradise of which they spoke.

Clothing, especially, was scarce but not as scarce for nomenklatura wives, who could buy much better fabrics than their non-nomenklatura counterparts. If chic is associated with Paris couture, for Russian couture the term, traditionally, has been "dowdy." This was partly because ideas were as limited as materials. Soviet women could not travel to Paris or Milan, and fashion magazines did not exist. There was no Russian *Vogue*. Another handicap was poundage. The unbalanced diet, heavy in fats and carbohydrates, the dullness of everyday life, and the emphasis on food and liquor at parties all tended to produce women inclined to plumpness at an early age. Though Raisa took more pains than most with her diet, photographs from those years in Stavropol show a woman who shared in the national fate.

Still, the nomenklatura wife stood out. She had to. As an official's wife, one of her duties was to project an attractive image, for which she even received a subsidy. But here, too, there were rules. The wife of a junior official could never dress better than the wife of a senior official. Nor could she look too European, too polished. But even for women of the nomenklatura, given the shortages, there was little danger of that.

If Soviet's women's clothes were dowdy, men's clothes were, by fiat, dull. Autumn, winter, and spring, Mikhail and his colleagues wore navy, black, or gray gabardine suits. Their long, heavy winter coats were also somber-hued, fastened at the neck with a small piece of fur. This and the ubiquitous fur hat added the only bit of dash to their look. In summer, the traditional uniform was a light gray suit, white shirt, and sometimes a straw hat, jaunty but functional: the summer sun could be brutal.

Nancy Reagan's comments to the contrary, Raisa dressed conservatively but well. In winter, she usually wore a quilted coat with a fur collar and fur trim on the sleeves, and a fur hat set at a provocative angle. She wore suede or fur-lined boots, but only ankle-high; knee-highs had yet to make their appearance in Russia, though the need was obviously there. Her everyday uniform was strictly business: a severely cut suit and a white blouse fastened at the neck with a brooch. For dressy evenings, she wore velvet or brocade. Only in summer did the uniform brighten. In keeping with the cheery colors of the countryside, women wore lightweight dresses in bright, vivid hues.

Because designer clothes were not available, most of the nomenklatura women's outfits were tailor-made, even their shoes. Small workshops existed in every region of the Soviet Union exclusively for the purpose of shodding the feet of the higher-ups. Proprietors came to know their clients' tastes and strove to please them, usually in direct proportion to their rank.

It was not until after the Twentieth Party Congress in 1956, and the subsequently more liberal politics, that style returned as a consideration in Soviet life. Contact with the outside world increased; interaction with neighboring Communist countries accelerated. By now, Moscow was entrusting even some regional officials with assignments abroad. Consequently, the Stavropol ruling class began to recognize that living standards in some Soviet satellite countries were better than theirs. They also noticed that the ordinary housewife was better dressed.

Among messengers from the outside world were the soldiers stationed throughout the Eastern bloc after World War II. Officers had been allowed to have their families with them, and their wives began to return to Russia with consumer goods that Soviet housewives could only dream of, "treasures" that aroused envy among their friends. But trends in the outside world were slow to come to Russia, even to its nomenklatura. Despite their greater ability to travel, where and with whom they traveled were limited. Nomenklatura wives spent their leave with nomenklatura husbands at mostly nomenklatura-dominated spas. Their families were treated in the same clinics, their apartments decorated with furniture from the same factories, and their children educated at the same privileged schools, whisked to and from in their fathers' official cars. Invariably, the younger generation in politics was recruited from among the offspring of the older generation, which made it even more difficult for outsiders to bring in some welcome fresh air.

Like everyone else of their rank, the Gorbachevs lived in a fairly standard house, which they distinguished in two ways: early in their marriage they acquired a piano, which their daughter, Irina, now played; and they continued to expand their collection of books, so that by now both their living room and bedroom looked like a library. They even functioned as one, with Raisa carefully supervising the lending and borrowing of books. Seldom did an evening pass without Raisa burying her head in a book; when she wasn't studying social and economic conditions in the hinterlands, nineteenth-century literature was her love.

For less cerebral forms of relaxation, the Gorbachevs fled south to their dacha on the Black Sea. All the party officials had their dachas there, each furnished according to rank. In keeping with Mikhail's position as first secretary of the City Komsomol Committee, the Gorbachevs' dacha was noticeably more modest than those of the party elders, but the family managed to graduate to more comfortable ones as Gorbachev advanced, which he did at reasonably short intervals.

In 1970, after fifteen years in Stavropol, he reached the highest rank in the provincial career structure: first secretary of the Regional Committee of the Soviet Communist Party. He was top man in a region approximately the size of South Carolina. Because the command structure of the provincial government was similar in function to the one in Moscow, his job could be compared to that of General Secretary of the USSR, though on a vastly smaller scale. In Stavropol, he was boss. Financially, he was accountable only to the Moscow leadership, who regarded him, like all regional first secretaries, as their executive manager in the area. Naturally, given reality, especially in sprawling Russia, regional chiefs tended to operate a bit more independently than that setup implies, and some were corrupt. But there is not even a suggestion that Gorbachev was. In general, he was thought to be an able administrator and, more than his predecessors, concerned about his region's welfare and growth.

He advanced and, by association, Raisa did too. She was now the highest-ranking wife, which naturally brought her increased attention—not all of it welcome. There was within the Soviet Union at this time an increasing drive for material affluence. This was largely in reaction to the self-denial preached by Stalin and the hardships imposed by the war, but now, with Stalin and the war a part of the past, people wanted comforts. And one way to achieve them was through corruption and bribes. Such abuses of power were particularly egregious during the Brezhnev era (1964–1982), when the tendency among the governing class to grab for themselves was not discouraged, with the result that corruption spread at an alarming rate.

But the people, too, wanted consumer goods. The extreme poverty of large segments of the Russian population existed in glaring contrast to the lifestyle of the elite, which only fed their desire. Some resorted to bribes, theft, and black marketeering. But even their efforts were petty compared to some of the henchmen of the elite who, to keep the luxuries flowing, organized themselves Mafia-style.

Once Gorbachev assumed the position of regional chief, his family was subjected to the importunings of sycophants, flatterers, and people promoting all sorts of unsavory schemes. Hardly a day went by that Raisa wasn't approached. But if the Gorbachevs ever yielded, it would indeed be shocking news. Their contemporaries considered them above such petty stuff, not merely clean but simon pure. The tendency, at least until recently, of sanitizing official biographies notwithstanding, it is likely that some of the hagiography on the Gorbachevs is true. In Pyatigorsk, for example, a middle-sized town not far from Stavropol, there was a factory renowned for its excellent pastries. It was the factory director's custom, at regular intervals, to take an assortment of his wares to the first secretary to "sample." Each time, Gorbachev is said to have sent them back with the message "Bon Appétit."

The Gorbachevs may have refused such gifts, but they did not renounce the comforts that went with their position. They now upgraded from an apartment to a roomy, two-story house on a quiet street downtown. Brick with stucco, the house was painted in the traditional cheery colors of southern Russia and ringed with a sunny, flower-filled garden. On the ground floor were a kitchen, pantry, dining room, and reception room; upstairs, bedrooms, Mikhail's study, and, at long last, a library. There is a picture of Raisa standing, characteristically, in front of a huge mass of books. She seems to be studying the rows with an informed eye. Within seconds, we know, she will confidently select one.

In the 1970s, though the export of oil and natural gas to the West, the amount of hard currency earned by the Soviet Union increased. This foreign exchange, plus the export of produce in return for merchandise, brought

Raisa spent the first two years of her life in a railway settlement in the small, obscure town of Vessolayarsk in the Altai Mountains.

Raisa Titorenko, a teenager with an expression out of an old Hollywood film.

The 1954 class photo of the Philosophy Department of Moscow State University.

Detail: fourth from left in the bottom row is Raisa Titorenko. In fact, long before the end of the course, Raisa took the name of Gorbachev.

Top, Raisa's room and her roommates in 1949. Raisa is in the middle (back row), on the right is Nina Lyakicheva, and on the left Ida Schulz.

Above, From left to right: Ida Schulz, Raisa, Siran Arut, Nina Lyakicheva, Khalida Siyatdinova.

1951: Raisa and her friend Nina Lyakicheva outside the children's home where Nina grew up.

Above left, Raisa and her friend Khalida Siyatdinova pose happily for Raisa's boyfriend, Oleg.

Above right, Spring 1950: Raisa, Khalida, and Oleg in a Moscow park.

Raisa with Tamara Rybina and Lydia Budyka.

Psychology student Raisa and law student Mikhail marry on
September 25, 1953.

Young Pioneers' Camp near Stavropol. From left to right:
Galina Vassilenko, teacher and wife of the Second Secretary
of the regional Komsomol committee; Lydia Budyka with her
husband, Alexander; Tamara Rybina, a doctor; Raisa and
Mikhail Gorbachev.

Irina Gorbachev (left) in April 1974, on her first trip abroad. She accompanied her father on his first trip to East Germany.

Irina, only daughter of the First Family of Stavropol, is married in May 1977 to Anatoly Verganski. The wedding is Stavropol's social event of the year.

Moscow, Alexei Tolstoy Street. The Gorbachevs lived on the seventh floor from 1968 to 1971.

Raisa (center) at a reception in the Palace of Congresses at the Kremlin, before her husband became General Secretary. On the left is Madame Ryzhkov, wife of the former Prime Minister, Nikolai Ryzhkov.

Raisa in East Berlin in October 1989 with Sandra, her youngest fan. Raisa's bodyguard is in attendance.

Right top, Mikhail and Raisa take a walk on the grounds of their dacha near Moscow.

Right bottom, Raisa has inspired in Mikhail her own love of the theater. After a performance they are photographed with the cast.

The Gorbachev clan at Mikhail's government dacha not far from Moscow. Front row, from left: Mikhail with his wife, Raisa; his granddaughter, Xenia; and his mother, Maria. Back row, from right, Maria's second son, Sasha Gorbachev; Irina, the Gorbachevs' daughter, and her husband, Anatoly Verganski; Luda, Sasha's daughter; and Sverta, Sasha's wife.

Left top, The election of People's Deputies in March 1989. Mikhail Gorbachev watches his wife with interest.

Left bottom, Mikhail and Raisa talk to workers at a collective farm in Uzbekistan.

February 1989: Mikhail and Raisa visit the central reactor of the nuclear installation at Chernobyl.

The famous Russian fashion designer, Slava Zaitsev.

A sketch by Zaitsev, dedicated to Raisa. "That is how I would dress Raisa Gorbachev," he declares.

Tamara Makeyeva, Raisa's favorite Russian designer.

December 1986: Raisa attends the showing of Yves Saint Laurent's collection. Raisa's personal secretary, Gusenkev, is on the right.

The Queen receives the Gorbachevs at Buckingham Palace on their second visit to London.

Rapprochement between the Kremlin and the Vatican, November 1989. Mikhail Gorbachev, then General Secretary of the Communist Party of the Soviet Union, Pope John Paul II, and Raisa.

December 1987: at a summit meeting in Washington, Nancy
Reagan and Raisa Gorbachev meet at the White House.

December 1989: the Malta summit. Raisa talks to President
Bush. Their respect for each other seemed to develop into a
mutual trust.

Looking back on twenty-five years of marriage: Mikhail and
Raisa in 1978.

Raisa opens her arms wide in greeting, a symbol of the glasnost that makes her so popular around the world.

the country an influx of Western goods. The beneficiaries of this consumer bonanza were, naturally, the members of the nomenklatura. In Stavropol, as throughout the Soviet Union, shops were opened to cater exclusively to them. Here, they could buy imported clothes, shoes, household appliances, stereos, and TVs, at prices subsidized by the state. Just how limited a group these beneficiaries were is illustrated by the statistics for Stavropol: out of a population of more than 100,000, not more than 100 people could use these shops.

More than half of these coveted consumer items came from Finland, which soon recognized the value of this vast untapped market to its east. Finnish clothes were sometimes of good quality, especially the jackets and coats, but the emphasis was on comfort and practicality, not style. Dresses, too, were exported, but often in synthetic fibers and in provincial styles. Even so, the demand for Finnish products remained keen. It was a mark of status to dress in imported clothes, even if they were only from Helsinki rather than Paris or Milan.

The supply of food also improved. Until the 1970s, it was customary for the nomenklatura housewife to buy her fruits, vegetables, and meat in government shops or on the free market. Now, she had a nicer place in which to do her marketing: "cadre shops," from which the rest of the population was banned. In rural areas, special food factories were established strictly for the purpose of supplying these shops. Quality was high and the prices unbelievably low. A pound of sirloin, for example, might cost a twentieth of what it would cost in an ordinary shop (and who could ever find sirloin?). Fruits and vegetables were also a fraction of their regular price. All these arrangements naturally added to the comfort of the nomenklatura, in Stavropol as much as in Moscow itself.

Medical care, too, in this "classless" society was administered strictly along class lines. With Gorbachev's ascent, his body was now the responsibility of the No. 4

Administrative Department of the Ministry of Health in Moscow. (In the provinces, this perquisite went only to first secretaries of district and regional party committees and their families.) Mikhail, Raisa, and Irina all received their annual comprehensive medical examinations at the Central Clinic on Rublev Street in Moscow, which could treat major problems like heart disease and cancer, as well as minor ones—eyeglasses for Mikhail.

Treatment at the clinic was associated with another privilege: access to a chain of convalescent homes and spas running from northern Russia to the sunny south coast of the Black Sea. Brezhnev-era officials were especially fond of spas—new ones were constantly being built—but Central Clinic clients generally preferred the older establishments, circa Stalin and earlier, not only for their more lavish appointments but for their desirable location in the quasi-tropical south.

In the early 1970s, the Gorbachevs for the first time spent their vacation at Oreanda, a select health resort in the Crimea. Even for hard workers like the Gorbachevs, the splendors of Oreanda made it impossible not to relax: the palatial building of yellow and rose-colored brick surrounded by a wide verandah, the cool and shady rooms, their balconies paved in marble, and roses blooming everywhere. Landscape architects had been deployed to create an idyllic scene: streams winding through gardens, summer houses garlanded with vines. In contrast to the beaches at Yalta or Sochi, where ordinary Russians took their holidays, the beach at Oreanda was spotless, and with charming amenities: little huts as shelter from the hot sun, and a beach café that served herbal tea and a delicious yeasty bun, called a "Kremlin cookie."

The sanatorium was staffed by only the most highly qualified doctors, nurses, physical therapists, and masseurs. The cuisine was not exactly hospital fare, offering some twenty-five entrées, any of which could be altered according to personal preference or the advice of a dietician.

The Gorbachevs usually spent four weeks in this Crimean nirvana, but they had other holiday options as well. Important provincial officials could now spend their leave as guests of Communist parties in Western countries, areas that had been off-limits before. Not long after Gorbachev's promotion, the family had its first glimpse of the outside world, though it was hardly representative; they spent a few weeks in a sanatorium on the Mediterranean that belonged to the Italian Communist Party. Such forays, however, were limited for security reasons, and officials were usually encouraged to spend their leave at Soviet spas or the more secure residences of their comrades in the Eastern bloc. Holiday homes in the Thuringian Forest of East Germany were particularly popular with the Moscow elite. One possible reason was the desirable merchandise that could be brought back from East Germany, long regarded as the consumer paradise of the Eastern bloc.

Though now allowed to travel abroad, Soviet officials during the Brezhnev era remained relatively isolated at home. The segregation between the public and top officials was enforced for obvious reasons. Given the difference in lifestyle, it was not considered prudent for the public to get too close a glimpse of nomenklatura life.

The Gorbachevs, too, were somewhat removed from the public. Consequently, the family was often the subject of rumors, especially Raisa, with her fancy diploma and impenetrable reserve. Toughened by her apprenticeship years, she simply shrugged off the petty gossip and concentrated on her family. Her isolation was mitigated by her work and extracurricular pursuits. She not only attended all opening nights in Stavropol, she also met with the theater managers and actors to discuss future plays. Her extensive knowledge not only of Russian drama but of international works made her more than a hanger-on. But in many cases, her ideas were impossible to put into effect by the local companies, whose resources, material and otherwise, were limited. The most gifted actors and directors looked for work in Moscow, Leningrad, Kiev, or the capitals of the Central Asian republics, not in stodgy Stavropol. Here, provincialism and bad taste reigned. People preferred soap operas and wooden dramas about the Revolution to the great Russian plays, and certainly to anything avant-garde.

Still, Raisa persevered, and in some ways succeeded in broadening Stavropol's taste. She managed to attract some name artists to the area, if only for guest performances, and to mount important exhibitions. During her involvement in the area's cultural activities, attendance at theaters and concerts went up.

As wife of the regional first secretary, she also took an interest in education. Conditions, she discovered in the course of her doctoral work, were appalling. Stavropol was hardly an intellectual beehive, but once you traveled outside its boundaries, social and cultural amenities disappeared at breathtaking speed. Some 40 percent of the families on collective farms lacked a proper education and, even as late as the mid-1960s, could barely read or write.

Partly to blame were working conditions. The typical agricultural laborer's day lasted fifteen hours, all of it consumed by back-breaking work. The absence of any labor-saving machinery meant that time to rest, let alone thumb through Plato—even Lenin—was virtually unknown. If people read anything at all, it was only the newspaper. Schoolchildren read books, but such knowledge as they acquired at country schools was lost once they, too, were caught in the unremitting grind of agricultural work.

Raisa's research convinced her that before educational levels could be raised, living and working conditions would have to be improved. The answer was not simply to fill the shelves of libraries with books. A much more active approach was needed. At Raisa's instigation, cultural excursions were arranged from outlying districts to city museums and places of historical interest. It wasn't exactly a cultural revolution but it was more than anyone else had tried, and in Stavropol today, they still credit Raisa with waking the region from its cultural torpor.

But possibly her greatest achievement during this time was wifely. There were greater peaks to climb than Stavropol, she reminded her husband, a conclusion he might have come to himself, but surely Raisa's prodding helped. Her faith in him helped, too: as his intellectual sparring partner, she was convinced that her husband had qualities that set him apart from the usual provincial administrator. He was intelligent, approachable and, above all, uncorrupt. It is doubtful that she had any particular goal in mind. She was just by temperament anti-complacency and, in terms of personal achievement, anti–status quo. Restlessly she sought fresh victories, and encouraged her husband to do the same.

It is tempting to consider what Raisa, with her intelligence and drive, would have done on her own had she been born a generation later and into a more egalitarian world. In any case, she performed brilliantly in her husband's behalf. She spent her free time summarizing not just technical books that would arm Mikhail with facts, but art and literature, to stimulate his mind. She prepared well-researched papers for him on a variety of topics, but what was more valuable were their private talks at home. Here, he was free to advance his opinions without fear of what the party or the bureaucracy would say, and to a listener who was his intellectual equal. When Mikhail went to work in the morning, it was with the zest and brainpower of two.

Even then, Raisa perceived that for a bold reformer, there were remarkable political opportunities ahead. And if he happened to have a helpmate who was ambitious and intelligent and far-seeing, that man might one day seize the initiative.

FOUR

Dr. Raisa Gorbachev

AMONG NANCY REAGAN'S complaints about Raisa was that she asked too many questions, that she lectured instead of talked. But just as clothes and society and helping her husband seemed to be Mrs. Reagan's chief interests, political and academic life were Raisa's. In fact, responsible for her boost into the world via gold medals and student grants, they were not merely her means of ascent, they were her core. In new or difficult or uncomfortable situations, that was the side of her that naturally came out. If she seemed to pummel Mrs. Reagan with questions about the art and architecture of the White House, it was not necessarily meant to discomfit her. As a lecturer, it was, after all, what Raisa did for a living.

Raisa had confidence—perhaps, according to some of her detractors, too much. But it was a confidence that grew slowly as she exposed herself to various challenges along the way. Pursuing her doctoral degree was one, and it gave her an expert grasp of the realities of Communist life.

Until the Gorbachevs moved to Moscow in 1978, Raisa kept her job in the department of philosophy at the Stavropol Agricultural Institute. She had made that choice when they first arrived. She could have studied for her doctorate in Moscow, but that would mean living apart from Mikhail. So, for the time, she settled for a party-designated job in Stavropol.

Her first job at the institute was to conduct seminars based on the philosophy lectures—unrewarding work since the students, there primarily to study agriculture, had to take Raisa's course but basically saw it as irrelevant. Would the cereal crop of a future farmer grow better if he studied philosophy? Would hens lay more eggs for an expert in Marxism-Leninism than for an ignorant farmer's wife? These were questions no one dared ask but they were on many students' minds.

It was an obstacle Raisa could handle. "Although Raisa had no experience as a teacher, she was so self-possessed in the lecture room that she gave you the impression that she had taught all her life," recalled Mikhail Chuguyev, a former colleague of Raisa's and now a friend. "Inspectors used to sit in on lectures at the institute quite often. Raisa always asked that her teaching methods be assessed by the inspectors as a matter of priority. She was remarkably cool and self-assured. Not that she was arrogant, rather she felt secure in her professional expertise. In the course of my academic career, I can't remember one staff member who did not sometimes have an off day, or occasionally come to lectures or seminars unprepared. Raisa was an exception to this rule. Raisa was always very conscientious and very ambitious. And another thing: almost without exception, the women students who finished college with a gold medal had attended her courses. They reached a significantly higher level of academic attainment than the other students. Although Raisa's attitude to her students was demanding, she enjoyed not just their respect but that of her colleagues on the teaching staff."

As she became more experienced, Raisa began to give lectures herself. Students and colleagues recall her ability to be interesting on a wide range of topics, presenting highly complex subjects in simple and demystifying terms. Even such abstract subjects as ethics and aesthetics, she enlivened with practical, real-life examples. But Raisa possessed another quality that her students did not appreciate as much: she pursued them, continuing to monitor their progress even after they left her class. And if she felt they were not living up to their potential, she let them know it. Such doggedness sometimes won her criticism and scorn but, as she was the wife of senior official Gorbachev, not to her face.

Every day, Raisa would arrive at the institute in her husband's staff car, which would pick her up again at the end of the day. In the final years of her stay in Stavropol, she even had a bodyguard, though not entirely out of need. In the Brezhnev era, the bodyguard was maintained largely for status. While not unheard of, violence against provincial authorities was rare.

The official car, the bodyguard—all made her seem even more remote. Yet she did have close friends, with whom she discussed her personal affairs. Their typical comment about the Gorbachevs: "how well they got along." But with strangers and colleagues she was much more discreet. She'd discuss work-related issues, talk shop—but not much else. Despite her attempt in later years to suppress all her personal photographs, some telling ones still exist. Even more telling are the ones that don't. During the period in which she worked as a lecturer, 1956 to 1978, there isn't a single picture of Raisa surrounded by students, giving a lecture, conducting a class. According to Professor Chuguyev, one of Raisa's idiosyncrasies was never to let herself be photographed with students. If she went to their parties, which she occasionally did, she invariably arrived after the picture-taking. "She always said she did not come out well in photographs," Chuguyev said. But she must have had other reasons, because she obviously photographs well.

Academic life had its lighter side, with the staff celebrating birthdays and holidays together. Though not a ringleader, Raisa was a participant and occasionally even let down her guard. "Nobody went to great expense for a party," Chuguyev recalled. "Usually the staff gathered in a lecture room for tea and cakes. Once, on her birthday, Raisa brought a little bottle of brandy with her, which in itself was something out of the ordinary, for as a rule Raisa did not touch alcohol. But it was the depth of winter in Stavropol, and most of the staff were more than keen to warm their innards."

During a tour of the lecture halls and seminar rooms in which Raisa taught, it is still possible to see the visual aids, newspaper clippings, and plans and sketches that she used. In one room is a writing table where she often worked. Students are sometimes led to this spot and told, "Sit here and perhaps one day you too will achieve something great."

In terms of the administration, her policy was to avoid controversy. She disliked squabbles and arguments. When they did happen, she always kept her cool. On one occasion, however, when she felt that her personal rights and those of her colleagues were being threatened, she decided to speak up. "It must have been in the mid-1970s," Professor Chuguyev recalled. "The college introduced the somewhat humiliating practice of making secret recordings of lectures, which were later evaluated by the governing body. Nobody liked the system, but everyone kept quiet because they did not want to antagonize the college rector. When Raisa discovered that her lectures had been secretly recorded, she was appalled. Part of her was deeply disillusioned, part furiously angry. She went straight to the rector to complain about this unlawful procedure, and, I might add, none of this took place discreetly. The rector tried to justify himself by pleading the existence of ministerial authorization for the secret recordings. Raisa did not believe him and wanted more precise information about this ruling, which she saw as an insult to the academic staff. Of course, the rector could produce nothing in writing, for there was no such authorization. Following this confrontation with Raisa, the unauthorized practice of recording lectures in secret came abruptly to an end."

Another colleague of Raisa's, Ekaterina Dysbal, recalled that Raisa took care not to stand out as a nomenklatura wife. "It was not unusual for wives of senior party officials to work at the institute," Dysbal said. "Some soon let it be known that they considered themselves superior to us, not just by their general attitude but also in the way they dressed. You know, when a woman changes her outfit several times in a day, that in itself comes across as quite a put-down to other women with only a couple of dresses in their wardrobes. Raisa was not condescending like some of the wives, though I can imagine she probably had as many different outfits as they had. At the institute, Raisa never dressed conspicuously, though this changed considerably later on when her husband became General Secretary of the party. As a lecturer, she almost always wore the same outfit, practically a uniform, a black suit and a white blouse. In winter, her favorite clothes were an orange mohair sweater and a simply cut black coat. The coat came from one of the shops 'for officials only' in Stavropol, and she had brought the pullover back from Italy when she went with her husband in 1972 to a celebration arranged by an Italian Communist newspaper."

Raisa used hardly any makeup, Dysbal said. "Just lipstick, which she put on unobtrusively—far less garishly than most Russian women. And she never gave herself airs. Neither was she very outgoing, but reserve is part of her nature; it was not expressive of her attitude toward us in particular."

When her husband was named first secretary of the Stavropol Regional Committee in 1970, Raisa, obviously concerned about the surge of lobbying activities that would ensue, made a preemptive strike. " 'Comrades,' " Dysbal recalled Raisa declaiming, " 'I have a large favor to ask you. Would you please not come to me with personal requests, appeals, or problems, in the hope that I can put them before my husband. I have no right to try to influence him. So please don't place me in an awkward position.' She made the situation clear to us once and for all, and so far as I know, none of her colleagues tried to obtain advantages through Raisa that were within her husband's power to grant."

As the clamor for favors indicated, connections with a high-ranking official might not have been a matter of life or death, but they could certainly improve one's lot. Somebody with "connections" experienced few bottlenecks in procuring services, and didn't have to stand in line for hours to obtain a piece of meat. How did you acquire these connections? If you didn't belong to a party chief's inner circle or some other privileged group, then you had to build up your own system, granting favors so you could demand them in return. You could even go so far as to become a paid informer of the police state. Given the hardship of everyday life in the Soviet Union, this was an ever-present temptation.

From the beginning, Raisa avoided close contact with people outside her immediate family. That way she could avoid their sad and desperate pleas, and their bribes. As for demanding favors for herself, the evidence suggests not only that she never did, but that she went to the opposite extreme: she was punctilious, adhering to rules even when no one cared whether she did. When her husband went to the Twenty-fourth Party Congress in Moscow, Raisa was invited to go too. A woman in her position might simply have taken the few days off. Raisa, however, chose to go by the book: formally asking the rector for an official leave and, when she returned, insisting on making up the lost time. Even when she stayed home because her daughter was ill, she made up the time she lost. Were her scruples exaggerated? Perhaps, but if she was morally impeccable, she was also shrewd: many a career had been wrecked by overstepping the bounds. Even in the United States, a president was being toppled for abuse of power.

Inevitably, her high standards and ultra-proper behavior invited a few practical jokes. One of these was a little cruel, the other very cruel. According to a participant in the first, "It was April 1 and Raisa was waiting anxiously for a response from the editor of a learned journal to an article she had submitted. For some reason or other, the reply was delayed. Some of us from the institute went to the post office with an envelope and persuaded one of the officials there to postmark it. As you know, every scholar likes to see his or her work in print. Inside the envelope was a letter we had written, in which the 'editor' stated that the article had been well liked and was going to be published. In addition, he expressed the hope that the author of such an outstanding article would give an account of her research to an international academic conference in Moscow. We quietly put the letter on her desk and watched for her reaction. Raisa was overjoyed. 'Comrades, my article has been accepted. Let's celebrate!' she said. We could restrain ourselves no longer. We all burst out laughing, and Raisa realized that we had dared to make fun of her. But she wasn't a spoilsport, and joined in the laughter."

The other prank occurred after Mikhail had already been made first secretary of the Regional Committee. Midway through a lecture, Raisa was suddenly summoned to the phone. "I saw her turn pale and sink into a chair," Ekaterina Dysbal recalled. "The caller had told her that her husband had been killed in a car accident." If the students hoped to see Raisa Gorbachev's more emotional side, they did.

After years as a lecturer, Raisa was promoted to professor of philosophy. She was delighted with the promotion, and viewed it as the reward for her unstinting hard work. But within a month she realized it was her husband's position and not her abilities that had induced the board to appoint her. She immediately went to the director and relinquished the chair. To her astonished colleagues, she explained that she did not much enjoy the administrative work a professorship would entail and had not set out to have an academic career, anyway.

Although she continued to lecture, she was also immersed in a new project, studying the living conditions of peasants in rural areas, which were not much different in Stavropol from those of other agricultural regions of the USSR: wretched. Earlier than most, the top officials in Stavropol seemed to realize that better production hinged on better living conditions. What they needed was a comprehensive report on the situation prepared by someone with an academic background. Raisa was selected for the task, which dovetailed beautifully with her doctoral work. The project appealed to her for another reason, as well. Her husband was eager for her to take on the assignment, since the region's agricultural production was among his many responsibilities.

In order to turn her research into a doctorate, Raisa needed to affiliate with a school. No college in Stavropol was equipped to supervise a doctorate in sociology, a relatively new and controversial field in the USSR. Consequently, Raisa decided to do her thesis under the aegis of the Lenin Pedagogical Institute in Moscow, considered to have the most progressive sociology faculty at the time.

While still a lecturer in Stavropol, she traveled to Moscow several times a year to present and discuss her findings with the Lenin Institute's leading social scientists. One of these, Spiridonovich Gott, a professor of philosophy, became a trusted mentor and later a close friend. (In his eighties, he still spends several weeks with the Gorbachevs in their dacha at Pitsunda on the Black Sea.) An academic who was active in international affairs, Gott has had an interesting life, especially during the war, when he was a trusted colleague of Vyacheslav Molotov, Stalin's famous foreign minister. According to Raisa's thesis adviser, Gott, who is one of the few remaining witnesses to the signing of the Hitler-Stalin pact, has in his possession a rare and valuable copy of the pact. He refuses, however, to make the document available. He is also said to possess a copy of Molotov's will, which supposedly contains valuable background information on Stalin's foreign policy decisions. Countless efforts to see the papers and interview Gott have met with a decisive *nyet*. His only comment: that it was a bad chapter in the history of the Soviet Union, and the Gorbachev family should not be linked with it.

Molotov was expelled from the Presidium in 1957, and Gott fell with him. However, Gott was sufficiently young and talented to recoup. Within a few years he returned to academic life, and in the 1960s was appointed professor of philosophy at the Lenin Pedagogical Institute. There, he personally supervised Raisa Gorbachev's doctoral work from 1965 to 1967, and headed the committee that would ultimately decide on whether to award the degree. Despite his age, he continues to be active in academic life. He is currently editor in chief of *Philosophy of Science,* a scholarly journal and professor of philosophy at the Soviet Academy of Sciences.

In 1964, Raisa was sufficiently advanced in her research to be accepted as a candidate for a doctoral degree at the institute. Eventually she passed her exams; all that remained was to finish her thesis. As her advisor, she was assigned Gennady Osipov, widely viewed as the "kingpin" of Soviet social science. The role of doctoral adviser in the Soviet Union is more clearly defined and important than in other countries. The adviser not only directs the student's work, but is held accountable for the "seriousness" of the approach and the student's attitude as well.

As a student of sociology both under and after Stalin, Gennady Osipov had a tumultuous career. Nowadays, he is viewed in a highly favorable light. The magazine *Sociological Research* credits him with initiating the first active social research in Soviet Russia and wresting sociology from the field of philosophy, under which it had been subsumed. Among his numerous works, considered fundamental to the field, are *Sociology in the USSR, The Sociologist's Handbook,* and *Marxist-Leninist Sociology.* On his initiative, the Soviets established the Sociological Institute within the Academy of Sciences, and appointed Osipov as its head.

Under Stalin, Osipov's plight, and the plight of sociologists in general, was considerably worse. "Sociology was considered a pseudo-science," said Osipov, who is a few years older than Raisa. "We had practically no academically trained sociologists. Stalin could not totally deny the legitimacy of sociology, with its concern for the structure of society. But he forcibly confined sociology within social philosophy, which meant, in effect, that philosophy took over. Philosophy deals with the analysis of society on a purely abstract plane. Any attempt by academics to examine social phenomena in concrete terms was regarded under Stalin as a divergence from Marxism-Leninism, as 'ideological sabotage,' part of a move to narrow social philosophy into positivism [which recognizes only empirical facts and rejects metaphysical abstractions]. To stand accused of ideological sabotage could cost a Russian his academic position and, for many, it had more terrible consequences.

"When the Stalin era came to an end, there was, under Khrushchev, a modest intellectual thaw, which enabled sociology to achieve some independence as a discipline. It was not a painless process. We sociologists had fierce opposition from an array of philosophers who were still prisoners of Stalinist dogma. They reopened the old charges of ideological sabotage and accused us of wanting to undermine the existing foundations of socialist society through our researches. The forces of academic conservatism tried to obstruct sociologists by any means possible, attempting to kill the profession while it was still in its infancy.

"Life was especially hard for young sociologists. Quite a number gave up, some for the second time, and those who did remain in sociology knew that they had only a minimal chance of attaining their doctorate. Only ten out of a hundred postgraduate students gained their Ph.D. in sociology, ever aware that they could be accused of being 'enemies of Marxist ideology.' The opposition to sociologists lasted well into the 1960s, so that it needed some courage to take up sociology and persevere with it in the face of all these adverse conditions."

Osipov himself was the victim of an anti-sociology wave in the 1960s. F. P. Trapesnikov, a high-ranking official in the education wing of the Central Committee, maneuvered to have Osipov stripped of his academic status. In one year alone, he received five official reprimands, enough to justify taking him to court. The trial, scheduled for the People's Court on Brest Street in Moscow, never actually took place. According to sources, the charges were withdrawn when it became apparent how absurd they were. Still, Osipov's credibility was not restored. He was put on a blacklist and for many years was forbidden to travel or participate fully in academic life.

It was in this sticky area that Raisa found herself. As her thesis advisor, Gott assigned her the controversial Osipov, who had been accused of "bourgeois thinking" and treated with undisguised contempt. But he was the right man for Raisa's work and, undeterred, she began her advanced studies, meeting with Osipov in the basement of the building at 16B Pishchevaya Street (a subsection of the philosophy faculty, the Department for Sociological Research had been condemned to this chilly space). Despite the dampness and, in winter, the frost on the walls, Raisa appeared for each session, eager to work. "A science which was without official status had no right to proper accommodations of its own," Osipov said. "But the optimism and intellectual curiosity of my colleagues overcame every obstacle."

Though Osipov had from the outset warned of the difficulties involved in working in the field, Raisa was interested only in moving on. Osipov was impressed both by her attitude and by what he deduced was one of her goals. "I sensed that the underlying motive for her commitment to sociology was to equip herself to support her husband in his career," he said. If not a motive, it was certainly a result. In fact, Mikhail accompanied her to these sessions on occasion, and added to the discussion his practical knowledge about conditions on collective farms. (No one had to guess when the Gorbachevs were in Moscow. Their black Volga staff car could be found parked in front of the dingy quarters on Pishchevaya Street.)

Raisa's work out in the fields of Stavropol produced the first doctoral thesis ever written by the wife of a Kremlin boss, though Osipov could not have known that then. Its title, even for the Soviet Union, was a little long-winded: "On the Formation of a New Pattern of Life for the Kolkhoz Peasantry, Based on Material Obtained Through Sociological Research in the Stavropol Region." (*Kolkhoz* = collective farmer.) Its goals were basically threefold: to analyze conditions on collective farms, to identify the obstacles to improving them, and to offer solutions. And then, in a more general vein, to analyze the effect of the social and economic conditions of the collective farm on the daily lives of the workers.

Western scholars who have read the thesis consider it "thoughtful," but not one that challenged ideological assumptions. This is only partly true. Though it did not criticize the basic tenets of the Marxist state, it did point up the failings of current policies, and could in some ways be viewed as a call for reform. In the first chapter, Raisa compares the consumer patterns of the pre-Revolution peasant with those of his collective-farmer counterpart, and points to particular problems that hold the present-day farmer back: poor roads, inadequate transportation, the inability of geographically scattered settlements to take advantage of public services that are far away, and the low degree of mechanization, a key factor in explaining the vast gulf between the farmer's arduous efforts and his meager results. Chapter Two focuses on intellectual and cultural life. Here, her data show that while the cultural aspirations of the workers had increased—greater library use, increased attendance at movies, concerts, plays—the means of fulfilling them had not. And finally, in Chapter Three, she examines patterns of marriage and social life, with some strong words on the special burdens of women. Among her numerous points: sheer drudgery weighs the women down. "The women collective farm worker who has to do her housework as well as carry out her duties on the farm faces not only a handicap to intellectual fulfillment but also an obstacle to the achievement of economic equality," Raisa wrote.

In her conclusion, Raisa writes that the quality of life in the village has vastly improved since the days of the Revolution. Economic and social life is on a higher plane. But in areas of health, education, and culture, the village is still decades behind.

The nature of her work hardly consigned her to an ivory tower. Increasingly, she spent her time on collective farms, where she not only compiled statistics but helped organize leisure activities and volunteered advice. As often as she could, she lectured about her work to important officials. Her aim: to drum up support for improving the amenities of village life, especially educational and cultural activities.

Raisa passed all her doctoral exams, both in the required subjects (dialectical and historical materialism) and the elective ones (history and English), with a "Very Good," the highest mark. In 1967, she was examined at the Lenin Pedagogical Institute on her thesis, or, officially, her "Dissertation for the Attainment of the Academic Title of Doctor of Philosophic Science." Among her examiners was Sergei Gurdyanov, now a professor of philosophy at Moscow State University. In his report, Gurdyanov praised her work as a serious contribution to the literature on rural problems, and one that didn't rely only on abstract speculation but on extensive empirical work. Others on the examining board agreed, and she was awarded her doctorate by a unanimous vote.

On the big day, Mikhail accompanied his wife to the institute and presented her with a magnificent bouquet—for "Dr. Raisa," he said. They ended the day on the usual Russian high note: a splendid banquet.

In 1969, Raisa published a shorter and more accessible version of her thesis, "Peasant Life on the Collective Farm: A Social Summary," and, in 1973, a pamphlet in Stavropol entitled "The Twenty-fourth Congress of the Soviet Communist Party and the Further Development of Socialist Culture." The Stavropol pamphlet marked her growing interest in culture. In the pamphlet, she advocated building or refurbishing 233 schools, opening at least forty boarding schools, and setting up an arts center in every village.

Lofty goals, and she would continue to pursue them after she left Stavropol. In 1986, she became a member of the governing body of the Soviet Cultural Foundation. "Few things occur now within the program of cultural restoration in Soviet Russia without her having some say in them," Professor Osipov observed. Merely her attitude has given Soviet culture a boost. "Influence on social and cultural life can, I believe, be exerted not only through books and articles or even through making practical proposals, but by personal attitudes and example," he said.

He also credits her with bolstering the status of his own beleaguered discipline. "Raisa Gorbachev is only one of a host of men and women who have made a significant contribution to *glasnost* and *perestroika* through their open support of sociology, which was this county's first socially progressive movement. Given the conditions of the time, her attitude was new, remarkable, brave—thoroughly impressive."

Asked about her contribution to improvements in the status of women, he was less roseate. "You must remember that the attitude of the Soviet general public to the wife of a top political leader is not the same as in the West. Raisa Gorbachev as a sociologist must be aware of this. If she were to make a well-publicized pronouncement on any subject, this would without doubt inspire an adverse reaction; it would be seen as an incursion into areas where she had no place. If, for instance, Raisa were to become active in a women's movement, you can be sure that critics would say there were many other problems far more deserving of her attention. I personally cannot accept all our traditions, but you make a large mistake if you ignore them."

Apparently, in 1988, Raisa had promised to take part in a symposium at the Academy of Sciences on the subject of the participation of women in society. "But something prevented her from attending, and we all regretted this very much," Osipov said.

As for her popularity or lack of it, Osipov offered

some explanations of why it was uneven and with whom. "First, you have a prejudice dating back to Stalin's time, the view that the wife of any government or party leader should remain apart from all social and political activity. Secondly, you have the age-old Russian tradition which still runs deep in the public consciousness, that a wife is ordained to occupy a lower rung on the social ladder than her husband. Today the large Muslim minority in the Soviet Union reinforces this patriarchal attitude."

In addition, Osipov said, many Soviet women had petit bourgeois values, so that when they saw the wife of a Soviet leader playing a conspicuous role in public life, they condemned her, even though her position might, in the long run, help them.

"I know that in America, for instance, if a president's wife dresses carelessly, if she's unfashionable or dowdy, she could cost her husband votes in the next election," he said. "In Soviet Russia, by contrast, if the wife of a high-ranking official appears in a variety of outfits, looking smart, she meets with severe disapproval, the more so because we have no tradition of elegant political wives. You only have to think of the wives of Khrushchev, Brezhnev, or Andropov. People say, 'How can that woman dress so well and look chic when, in this country, we don't have enough clothes to go around?' "

In some ways, even pursuing her doctorate was regarded as hubris. Some people accused her of trying to "grab the limelight" and, as Dr. Raisa, she was the subject of considerable spite. "Some of our traditions are primitive and barbaric, and I think it will take quite some time to adjust Russian modes of thinking and bring them into line with European culture," Osipov said. "Will Raisa reap the benefits of such changes? Here, I'm a bit of a pessimist. Regrettable as it may be, I believe, as so often, the Bible is right, and a prophet is not without honor except in his own country."

FIVE

Return to Moscow

IN STAVROPOL, the intelligence and energy of Mikhail Gorbachev continued to reap results. Under his leadership, even the agricultural economy, a problem everywhere else in the Soviet Union, improved. But he was also helped by fate. His predecessor in the top post in Stavropol, F. D. Kulakov, was transferred to Moscow as head of the agricultural department of the Central Committee, giving him an ideal position from which to advocate for his successor. But in 1978, at age sixty (hardly old in Soviet politics), Kulakov died suddenly. No member of the party leadership attended his funeral, which gave rise in Moscow to rumors—personal rifts, maybe even suicide. With no well-known party leaders attending the funeral, the delivery of the oration was assigned to a party official almost unknown outside his region: Mikhail Gorbachev.

But neither Kulakov's praise nor even Gorbachev's own abilities would in themselves have assured him of a summons to Moscow. Another factor shortened his route. Yuri Andropov, the powerful head of the KGB at the time, suffered from serious kidney problems and often sought treatment in the health resorts around Stavropol. Both he and Premier Alexei Kosygin, also a familiar visitor to the region's spas, were frequent guests of the Gorbachevs, and found much to admire in Raisa. It was unusual to find someone of her charm, personality, and intelligence as a regional official's wife. Long walks with Andropov's wife, on which Raisa talked about her beloved Moscow, helped to strengthen the friendship between the women, too. Sensitive hosts, the Gorbachevs maintained that delicate balance between friendship and discretion. Naturally their visitors were impressed. It would be hard to imagine a more synchronized team than Raisa and Mikhail.

Largely due to Raisa, the Andropovs decided to spend their vacation with the Gorbachevs in Kislovodsk in 1977. In keeping with protocol, the Andropovs were under the care of Red Stones, an exclusive sanatorium, and stayed in their dacha in a nature reserve. The Gorbachevs stayed at nearby Blue Stones, a sanatorium of appropriately lesser cachet. But the two couples met for walks every day and, by all accounts, got along extremely well.

On November 28, 1978, *Pravda* announced that Mikhail Gorbachev had been appointed to the Central Committee (the details of his selection were vague). In many ways it was a measure of Raisa's achievement, too. "Raisa had decided that the most important thing in her life was to help her husband in every possible way," her friend Lydia Budyka observed. "Their relationship is so close that Mikhail always likes to know that she is within call, so that they can discuss things together. She is a friend as well as a wife." She had an intuitive grasp of what was right for her husband. That she resented playing second fiddle hardly seems to be the case: his success was hers. What was remarkable about her and many women of her generation is that they managed to do both: bolster their husbands' careers and establish their own as well. Raisa was well equipped for the role assigned her. She was ambitious, intelligent, and free of inordinate amounts of self-doubt. If she was opportunistic and calculating, it was to a reasonable point and not beyond.

The Gorbachevs set off for Moscow in late 1978, following Mikhail's new appointment. Irina, who was now a pediatrician, and her husband Anatoly, a surgeon, made the move with them. The Gorbachevs' new home was a five-room apartment on Alexei Tolstoi Street in a party-owned building reserved specifically for Central Committee members.

As usual, the size and grandeur of their apartment corresponded with their rank. Far more luxurious than their house in Stavropol, the new apartment was nowhere near as grand as the houses of members of the Politburo. For the elite, the comforts of home had improved dramatically in recent years. In the late 1970s, Western architecture and aesthetics started cropping up in Moscow, at least in its official wards. The higher the official, it seemed, the more Westernized his home.

Shura Paradina had made railway cars into homes; her daughter, too, was resourceful at setting up camp. Flowers and potted plants, pictures on the walls, handsome appointments gave her homes a personal touch. A virtual nomad as a child, she took root wherever she lived. No place was ever regarded as a temporary billet, even if temporary billet is exactly what it was.

Of course, the apartment on Alexei Tolstoi Street didn't need much fixing up. From its balcony, you could peer over Moscow's many parks, old streets, and historic buildings. And then Raisa had help—some of Moscow's leading designers, using equipment and materials from the West. The result was an elegant interior, far more elegant than the exterior. From the outside, the building in which the Gorbachevs lived looked like almost any other Moscow building, a deliberate effort at conformity. Only the sentry box in front indicated that it wasn't Ivan Ivanovich (John Doe) who lived there, lest Comrade Ivanovich get any ideas.

During the brief time in which they lived on Alexei Tolstoi Street, the Gorbachevs had interesting, if not the most respectable, neighbors. Around them were buildings that belonged to the KGB, but also in this KGB ghetto was the famous "No Name" restaurant, a gathering spot for criminals, speculators, and no few lowlifes with famous last names, among them Brezhnev's daughter, whose innumerable affairs and shady dealings made her notorious in later years.

The Gorbachevs lived in the apartment on Alexei Tolstoi Street for only two years, but to this day it remains unoccupied. According to one source, this was the family's wish, though it is a difficult one to fathom, given the grave housing shortage in Moscow, where families of six or eight are crowded into two or three rooms, three generations together, the grandchildren having no hope of a home of their own. When I told some Soviet friends about the Gorbachevs' untenanted apartment, they weren't particularly interested, preoccupied as they were with problems closer to home. They had just been standing in line for six hours to buy meat. Such paradoxes are a fact of Soviet life.

At the end of 1980, Gorbachev was made a full member of the Politburo, marked by another move, this time to an apartment on Shchusev Street—Politburo country, i.e., very nice indeed. The architectural style of this block was pure Brezhnev—heavy concrete, huge windows, imposing entrances. Only the most privileged people in Moscow society lived there, among them Valentina Terechkova, the Soviet cosmonaut, and Brezhnev's daughter, Galina. The cosmonaut is still there, but not Galina. As part of the clean-up initiated by Gorbachev, it was revealed that Galina and her husband Yuri Churbanov, a general and first deputy of the Ministry of the Interior under Brezhnev, had amassed a fabulous personal fortune from smuggling and corruption. They had also taken trunkloads of valuables and irreplaceable works of art out of the country, and otherwise enriched themselves at the Soviet people's expense. It was reported that $200,000 in cash and a million dollars' worth of jewels were found in their apartment. Churbanov was sentenced to ten years' imprisonment in 1988. His wife's sentence, partly self-imposed, was even worse: stripped of all her privileges, she became an alcoholic and now resides in a psychiatric hospital.

With the move to Moscow, Raisa gave up most of her academic work and put aside the professional opportunities open to her. Instead, she immersed herself in her husband's work. She read new reports and summarized the relevant ones for his benefit. She kept him supplied with a steady stream of data. Her own career had merged with his: she was now her husband's chief aide.

PART TWO

SIX

Life in the Leadership

GORBACHEV'S APPOINTMENT as General Secretary was officially announced on March 11, 1985. He was the eighth General Secretary since Lenin. Andrei Gromyko, the veteran Soviet diplomat, said in explanation that Gorbachev had a charming smile and exceptionally strong teeth, but that may have been sour grapes: in fifty years of service, Gromyko had never been offered the job.

Naturally, the family's lifestyle improved. In the highest echelons of the Soviet hierarchy, the material benefits are endless: luxurious houses, gourmet food, a wide range of domestic help from chefs to chauffeurs. And to get away from it all, holidays at party-exclusive resorts on the Black or Baltic Sea.

Curiously, salaries lag behind. Politburo members are paid only 1,200 rubles a month (about $670), far higher than the average worker's pay (234 rubles a month, or $130) but not as high as people in certain quasi-capitalist jobs. The owner of a successful cooperative restaurant, for example, might make 5,000 to 8,000 rubles a month ($2,800 to $4,500). And important scientists, writers, and artists all earn more than top politicians.

But then there are the hidden extras, one of which is purchasing power. The same ruble in the hands of a Politburo member buys nicer things than it does for the Soviet housewife. Raisa and her peers can shop abroad or at home in exclusive shops. But even had she somehow procured a million rubles, Comrade Housewife would be limited to the thinly stocked shelves of Soviet stores.

The privilege factor is most evident in the area of housing. Even the most prosperous Soviet citizen has no chance of acquiring one of the spacious apartments or houses in which the leadership live. This issue was broached, for the first time, under Gorbachev. It wasn't that the Gorbachevs lived any better than their predecessors; it was just that under *glasnost* the people felt they had the right to criticize the privileges of the elite. Among the more heated interchanges took place at the Congress of People's Deputies in March 1989. In reply to angry interrogators, Gorbachev explained: "We have a house in town. Neither I nor members of my family have a private dacha." (Which is true. The luxurious dacha the Gorbachevs live in, like the White House, is owned by the state.)

"In consideration of their duties," he continued, "government dachas are put at the disposal of senior government members. The dacha allocated to the General Secretary of the Central Committee of the Communist Party and the President of the Supreme Soviet fulfills a particular function and is equipped accordingly. It can accommodate a meeting of the Politburo or of the Supreme Soviet, or a reception for heads of state from other countries. It has an office, a library, and a communications center with the most up-to-date equipment.

There are also technical installations, which are essential to the executive function of the chairman of the Soviet Defense Committee. Only a portion of the accommodations at the dacha is for the private use of the family."

His reply, though lengthy, was not exactly complete. What about the sauna, the swimming pool, the conservatory with exotic plants—are they for the benefit of the state? In fact, many question why Gorbachev, the catalyst behind so much reform, has been slow to address the issue of privilege among the elite. In opposition circles, the rumor is that the poor boy from Privolnoye is loath to relinquish his privileges, and so is his wife. Nonetheless, in even addressing the issue, Gorbachev is at least considered more candid than most, and if his lifestyle seems more exciting than that of his predecessors, it is not because he and his wife are any more decadent, only more hip.

Where do the Gorbachevs live? Since 1985, they've spent most of their time in their dacha (an imposing country estate and not a "weekend cottage," as the term is sometimes rendered in the West). Their dacha, like those of their colleagues, is on Rublev Avenue, a beautiful, romantic, tree-lined street. Its narrow two lanes, only a few kilometers from dirty, stifling, industrial Moscow, are off-limits to traffic (except for the Volgas, Chaikas, and Zil limousines carrying the elite). Gorbachev travels in the center of a long procession of black and chrome: a KGB Mercedes, one or two black Volgas, two Zils, a Zil station wagon, which is really an ambulance, and a black Volga completing the line. (The two Zils in the middle are to confuse onlookers; with their blackened windows, no one can tell in which one Gorbachev is riding.)

Gorbachev's son-in-law, Anatoly, drives a gray Mercedes; Raisa has a Chaika for personal use, though neither she nor Irina can drive. Few women in the Soviet Union have driver's licenses. But even if Raisa could drive, she would not be permitted to, and neither, for security reasons, would Mikhail. Chauffeurs convey them everywhere, and usually with an army of guards. Occasionally, however, they sneak off alone, as they did one July morning. The night before, after an unusually late session of the Supreme Soviet, Gorbachev invited his colleagues back to his house for dinner. The fleet of Zils deposited their passengers at the house and, when dinner was done, picked them up and departed toward Rublev Avenue ("Dacha Row"). The next morning, a Saturday, a lone Zil with no escorting convoy arrived at the entrance of the house and Gorbachev himself, looking very jolly in a light summer suit, stepped out and disappeared into the house. Within a quarter of an hour he reappeared with Raisa, gay and summery in white linen. They were walking arm in arm, laughing. As soon as he spotted them, the chauffeur leaped out to open the door, but Gorbachev waved him aside. The Gorbachevs climbed in and the Zil sped off. There wasn't a security guard in sight.

The dacha, where the Gorbachevs spend most of their time, is fairly convenient to their various destinations, a half-hour drive from the Kremlin, the Central Committee headquarters, and the Cultural Foundation, where Raisa works. Turning off Rublev Avenue, a narrow asphalt road leads to the dacha, surrounded by an electronically monitored fence. Inside, the battalion of guards (all courtesy of the KGB) is divided into two groups, an external group, twelve guards who escort Raisa and Mikhail on their journeys in and out of town, and an internal group, who guard their various homes—in lurid security terms, "protecting the target." The area between the fence and the house is monitored by an electronic warning system. Should anyone try to approach the house, security men and guard dogs will pounce.

These are not ordinary security guards but professional soldiers from the KGB 9th Corps, who protect not only Politburo and Central Committee members and their families but candidates for these positions as well. Even the domestic staff are more likely to have graduated from the KGB than a hotel management school or the Cordon Bleu. If it sounds a little sinister, it is, but then one legacy of Stalin's paranoia is that there are fewer assassinations of top officials in the Soviet Union than elsewhere in the world.

Other aspects of dacha life are less martial. Once past the gate, you drive along a road surrounded by lush grounds, pine and spruce and carefully tended shrubs. There are flower beds, too, some planted in the precise, symmetrical shapes of English gardens. Raisa, who loves flowers, supervises the garden and is always in search of new plants. On a state visit to Cuba, she continually demanded from her interpreter the names of plants and which if any of these spectacular tropical blooms would survive the Russian winter. In her own garden, she grows less exotic species but with no less skill: tulips, asters, gladioli—even roses, which, as a rule, do not flourish in town. Because the Russians grow so many, the Germans call lilacs the "Russian rose," and they are abundant here, too, in white and purple profusion around the house, their scent especially provocative in May and June. What Raisa does manage to bring home from her trips abroad are grown in the dacha greenhouse, along with other exotic fare: gherkins and pumpkins, and flowers that Muscovites rarely see: roses, carnations, crocuses, and orchids. The dacha even has its own orchard—apple, pear, and cherry trees. Raspberries and red currants flourish here, too. Roaming the grounds are peacocks, pheasants, and guinea fowl. Imported from southern Russia, they have evidently been "re-educated" to survive the cold.

The main building is connected to others through a series of covered walks. One of these leads to a low, one-story structure that houses a sauna and swimming pool. In summer, the walls can be retracted—one flick of a switch and a swimmer can find himself doing laps in view of the garden. Around the pool are Finnish wicker chairs and lounges with floral-patterned cushions. The color of the pool water can be changed—sea green, deep blue—and there are floodlights at night. It's no mystery, then, why in this Communist Eden few party officials can muster the courage to relinquish such perks.

The sauna, too, is grand. For some twenty years, ownership of a Finnish sauna has been a status symbol in the Soviet Union. Senior functionaries built saunas in their dachas and town houses, until the point was reached when a family without a sauna of its own was a disgrace to its name. The Gorbachevs' sauna is so spacious that no small part of the Central Committee could, and maybe does, caucus here. Inside the anteroom, which is paneled in light wood, are a huge stove, a large wooden table, and benches and stools from Finland.

On the other side of the house, a walkway leads to more functional quarters: kitchen, larder, and utility rooms. The kitchen is large and well equipped (appliances from the West). Beyond are the servants' sitting room, dining room, and TV lounge. Except for the television, the whole scene could be from *Upstairs, Downstairs,* with its two classes living so closely but in such different worlds.

Like many dachas, the Gorbachevs' was built during the time of Stalin. The dictator was fond of Le Corbusier, and many of the dachas are reminiscent of the Swiss architect's cool, functional style: large, uniform, rectangular buildings with handsome verandahs in back. (Le Corbusier himself worked on projects in the Soviet Union, including the Hotel Moskva, not far from Red Square.) In other ways, however, the buildings are pure Russian: brick with yellow stucco, and roofs of dark green metal with flat areas for sunbathing.

The cost of building the Gorbachev dacha was about 6 million rubles. The complex includes a helipad, a communications center, and apartments for official guests. In the residential quarters, aside from the usual living room, dining room, and bedrooms are a private screening room and a billiard room. Most of the interior is decorated in the style favored by Stalin: wood paneling, massive leather furniture, and heavy drapes. The furniture (all from the Lux factory in Moscow, where it was made in the time of Stalin), it is safe to assume, does not reflect the current occupants' taste. On the oak floors are the traditional "Kremlin runners"—raspberry-red strips of carpet with green borders and fine, sand-colored stripes, named for the place where they originally appeared. And everywhere there are flowers, as if the Russians have to make up for indoors what the weather deprives them of outdoors. In the dacha's conservatory, even palm and orange trees bloom—an exotic sight in this northern capital.

Raisa's comment on visiting the White House (and it distressed her hostess) was that it seemed a bit chilly—less a home and more a "museum." Her comment could apply to the Gorbachev dacha as well, and probably for the same reason: like the White House, it belongs not to its occupants, mere tenants of fleeting history, but to the state. Some Soviet officials with a more reformist bent— Boris Yeltsin, for example, onetime party maverick who is now president of the Russian Republic—find such party-bestowed luxury a scandal. Apparently the Gorbachevs don't. But what life is really like in this mini-Kremlin is hard to say. Unlike in America, where presidential cooks and First Ladies' secretaries can retire to write best-selling memoirs about life at the top, employees at the Gorbachevs' dacha are constrained to be more loyal. Upon starting employment, they must sign a pledge that they will never reveal any details of dacha life, even after they leave. This applies to each of the four categories of employees: gardeners and grounds workers; plumbers, carpenters, and electricians; kitchen staff and servers; and the housekeeping staff. Everyone reports to a chief steward, who, like all his underlings, must be thoroughly investigated before being hired.

Among the more personal touches in the Gorbachev dacha or, in Yeltsin's phrase, this "marble tomb," is Raisa's collection of Meissen porcelain. The collection is her personal treasure, and even to dust the vases or figurines, a housekeeper must be authorized. Once, during a state trip to Cuba, Raisa spotted a familiar vase in a museum in Havana. Much to the consternation of the curator, she lifted it from its plinth and sighed, "Ah, Meissen." She then launched into one of her famous lectures, on all she had learned about Meissen during her tour of the Meissen factory in East Germany, where most of her collection is from. Her oldest piece, however, is from the Gardner factory in St. Petersburg (now Leningrad), where the famous Kuznetzov porcelain was produced for the Romanov tsars. Like the tsars, Raisa has a passion for objets d'art.

ONCE THE GORBACHEVS moved into their dacha, a sore bargain was struck. In exchange for luxury and privilege, they gave up a certain amount of autonomy in their private life. No sphere was too trivial for the government to play a role in. The pleasure of browsing through nomenklatura shops was no longer theirs. Now, all their provisions were ordered by telephone and delivered to their house, courtesy of the state. Even what they ate was not entirely their choice. Raisa could plan her family's meals but, by order of the Politburo, a dietitian had final say over what she could and could not serve. As for cooking, that pleasure was denied to her too, for reasons as sinister as they were insulting: theoretically, even the General Secretary's wife might wish to poison him. All the Gorbachevs' food was cooked in a kitchen under KGB supervision and tested by human guinea pigs known as "mushroom men" (since presumably everyone would be quick to know if they ate, say, poisonous mushrooms). No fewer than ten people have to testify with signatures and rubber stamps that the food is safe. For Raisa, who loved to cook and often collected recipes from her colleagues at the Stavropol Agricultural Institute, this restriction must have been especially hard to bear.

Even the General Secretary's mother was not exempt. During Gorbachev's visit to his hometown of Privolnoye in 1988, "Baba Manya" (Grandma Manya), as he calls her, was not allowed to stew a chicken or roll blinis for her son. "Please, let me prepare a meal for my son," she beseeched the KGB, but to no avail. In the same unvarying routine, the food was prepared in KGB kitchens, sampled by KGB men, and delivered, via the mushroom men, to Gorbachev's untouched plate.

Of course, there were some privileges Raisa still retained, like putting through her daily food order either to a food warehouse in Tranovski Street or the food department at GUM. Though not exactly Bloomingdale's, the Moscow department store familiar to tourists still supplies the elite with exceptional food, though nowadays, not without grumblings from the masses. Under *glasnost,* people have become especially critical of the nicer ways in which party officials shop and eat. And as supplies decrease, their resentment naturally grows, which is why, unlike the American public, they are less than enthusiastic about state-directed anti-tobacco and anti-alcohol campaigns. If they can't have meat, at least let them have their vices. In 1989, for example, sugar rationing to curtail the production of bootleg liquor was imposed as part of Gorbachev's anti-alcohol campaign. At the time, a number of jokes circulated throughout Moscow. For example: "Have you seen the latest photo of Raisa?" one Muscovite asks another.

"No. Why?" the other replies.

"It shows her weeping bitter tears."

"That's not possible."

"Oh yes it is. She lost her sugar coupons."

The anecdote is delivered in a sarcastic voice, for obviously the wives of party officials don't lose coupons because they don't receive them—just sugar, all they want.

As long as the wives of high-ranking members of the government and party don't have to shop themselves, don't have to line up for hours at the collective-farm market, people complain, conditions will be slow to improve. Before Gorbachev made any changes, people were particularly affronted by the so-called health-food stores, distribution centers of rationed goods for officials only—one of them conveniently near the Kremlin. From midday on, narrow Tranovski Street was choked with Volgas and Chaikas belonging to the wives of senior officials. Under Gorbachev, the system has been changed, though not necessarily improved. Bigwigs can still purchase special provisions, but in more clandestine ways. And the numbers who maintain this privilege have been reduced: only members and candidates for the Politburo and secretaries of the Central Committee can stock up. This curtailment, partly good politics, was also a matter of economic necessity. Even for party officials, certain foods were getting harder to obtain.

Health care, too, is superior for the upper ranks, and has been even from the earliest days of the Soviet state, when top officials and their families had their own personal physician, usually a professor. And when they became sick, they were sent to the Kremlin Hospital, a three-story gray building on the corner of Tranovski Street and Kalinin Prospect, also near the Kremlin. The names of the wards commemorate some of its more illustrious patients—Stalin, Khrushchev, Brezhnev—but not those who, undoubtedly, had less pleasant stays. It was here that the victims of police brutality (rubber truncheons, electric shock) were taken for "treatment." The interior hasn't changed since the 1930s—oak-paneled halls, Kremlin runners, the heavy leather furniture that Stalin favored, and massive doors that seem more appropriate for a fortress than a hospital. Still, they insure privacy, which explains why prisoners were sent here in the past and why today the very highest officials can be treated in absolute secrecy.

Another health center for VIPs is farther from downtown but more convenient to the Rasory (the neighborhood where all the dachas are). Here, in the middle of a forest surrounded by a heavy security fence, Yuri Andropov, one of Gorbachev's predecessors and his mentor, spent his last days, November 1982 to February 1984, suffering from kidney disease, Mrs. Andropov at his side.

Gorbachev has of yet had no need of all these impressive facilities. As the first recent Soviet leader in middle age, he is in good health. Most of his medical care consists of routine monitoring and preventive techniques. In addition to a personal physician, he is treated by a physiotherapist and a masseur. And Raisa is fairly vigilant in matters of health. Both she and Mikhail do calisthenics every day; even during their vacations in Pitsunda, their daily regimen doesn't change.

Which doctor treats which official is, of course, a function of the political winds. The No. 4 Administrative Department of the Ministry of Health, which is responsible for the medical welfare of the leaders, was in the Brezhnev era the domain of E. I. Chazov—"our specialist and friend," as Brezhnev called him at a medal-awarding ceremony at the Kremlin. But as Brezhnev became discredited, so did his various henchmen, and his physician, too, lost clout. Although he no longer treats the leadership (the Gorbachevs' doctor is Vladimir Yarigin, director of the No. 2 Medical Institute in Moscow, where Irina worked), Chazov remains an influential man. He was, for a period, minister of health under Gorbachev and is deputy chairman of "Doctors for Peace," a group that campaigns internationally against nuclear and chemical weapons. In fact, it was Chazov who proposed that Gorbachev seek the advice of Dr. Robert Gale, a leading U.S. authority on radiation effects, who eventually went to Chernobyl.

There are a few exceptions to the domino theory regarding public officials and their aides. A. T. Medvedyev, for example, was Brezhnev's bodyguard and is now Gorbachev's. Perhaps he is one of those civil servants more astute than their employers about surviving the vagaries of political life.

Only once was a Gorbachev seriously ill. In 1966, Raisa suffered from abdominal pains but was too busy to seek treatment. One night, while dancing at an official reception with Mikhail, she suddenly turned deathly pale. Her husband took one look at her and immediately drove her to the regional hospital in Stavropol. There she was promptly diagnosed (a burst appendix) and operated on at once. In this case, belonging to the nomenklatura may indeed have been a matter of life and death. Not all emergencies are treated so quickly or so well.

Party leaders aren't the only ones who receive special medical care. Major institutions such as the Academy of Sciences, the Writers' Union, and individual government ministries all have their own clinics. The standard of care is much higher here than at the polyclinics and hospitals where ordinary citizens go. Under the Soviet constitution, all citizens have an equal right to state-supported health services—but just how much support varies widely. Ten to fourteen times as much money is spent on a patient in Moscow's No. 4 Hospital, for example, than on one in the public hospital only a few yards away. Such privileges have been a target of public criticism, but not ones on which, so far, the leadership has been willing to yield.

Certain egalitarian impulses have survived the long and disillusioning aftermath of the Bolshevik Revolution. When the Soviet government was transferred from Petrograd to Moscow in 1918, Lenin and his closest colleagues moved into the Kremlin, but not into the magnificent rooms that had been occupied by the tsar; they took over the more modest quarters used by the tsar's staff. To this day, no General Secretary of the Soviet Communist Party has ever occupied the tsarist suites. In the 1920s and 1930s, Stalin and his staff, following Lenin, continued to live in the service quarters. But slowly, they started wandering into less proletarian realms: a splendid six-story mansion on Tranovski Street which before the Revolution had been home to poets, novelists, and actors (members of the bourgeoisie). But in keeping with the Bolshevik spirit, they stripped the house of its trappings of class, consigning the fine furniture and paintings to government warehouses and furnishing the place in dreary Kremlin style. Some of the rooms were left empty, used only by Central Committee officials summoned by Stalin from out of town. Others were occupied by the Red Army head and important ministers. The outer wall of the mansion pays tribute to all these worthies; plaques bear the names of the various Soviet families who have lived there.

Following Stalin's death in 1953, housing policies changed along with everything else. Soviet leaders and their families moved out from the shadow of the Kremlin and into the more comfortable houses in the Sparrow Hills (renamed the Lenin Hills, though it's not clear that Lenin would approve). This area, on the banks of the Moscow River in southwest Moscow, is one of the most beautiful in the city, and private too. High stone walls protected the occupants from prying eyes. With their honey-colored exteriors and dark green roofs, the houses resemble dachas.

Khrushchev's downfall in 1964 and the rise of Leonid

Brezhnev brought yet another change. Brezhnev decided it was "undemocratic" for party leaders to live in such large houses, and so more modest housing was provided in the quiet streets of central Moscow. These houses may have been more democratic but, with their ten to fifteen rooms, were hardly typical of the cramped apartments in which most Soviet families lived. (In 1980, Gorbachev and his family moved into one.) Meanwhile, the houses in the Lenin Hills remained unoccupied, though occasionally they were used to accommodate overseas guests. In terms of facilities, they are still first-rate. In the nearby Hall of Receptions is a sports complex with two tennis courts, physiotherapy rooms, and a swimming pool.

In the mid-1970s, the number two man of the Brezhnev era, Premier Alexei Kosygin, decided to return to the Lenin Hills. He moved into one floor of a new three-story house, complete with sauna, conservatory, pool, and roof garden. Two senior officials occupied separate apartments on the other floors.

At the end of 1986 the Gorbachevs moved into a new house on Kosygin Street in the Lenin Hills. The three-story building, made of concrete with yellow plaster, is surrounded by iron railings and a narrow lawn and, because this is Raisa's house, there's a little flower bed in front. Compared to the main thoroughfares of Moscow, Kosygin Street is quiet and peaceful, with stately old trees. The backs of the houses afford a superb view of Moscow. Turn-of-the-century Muscovites cantered along the bridle paths and drove their carriages here. In summer, today's residents like to relax in the green parkland at the foot of the hills, which stretches for several miles along the banks of the Moscow River. For the Gorbachevs, the Lenin Hills have special meaning. Here was where they spent some of their happiest days as students and as newlyweds.

On the lower level are the security guards' quarters,

communications offices, a kitchen, and a sitting room for chauffeurs. On the first floor are rooms for "medical" treatment—a massage room, sauna, and indoor pool. On the second floor are two apartments occupied by other VIPs, and on the third floor, the apartment where all the Gorbachevs reside: Raisa, Mikhail, Irina, her husband Anatoly, and their children, Xenia and Anastasia. On their evenings at home, the family sometimes watches European and American TV programs.

The elite may not have given up their privileges, but clearly some things have changed, or so it seems to an amateur sleuth. While strolling past the Gorbachev house with a Russian friend, I took out my camera, found a good position, and started shooting. Chattering excitedly, I failed to notice that my friend had disappeared. Long before I had, he realized that heading in our direction was a security guard with a machine gun. I quickly held out my hand and explained who I was. The guard's response was not what I expected. "Take as many pictures as you want," he said. "Mikhail Sergeyevich is at the Kremlin at the moment, and Raisa Maximovna is at the dacha. Their daughter came back to the house an hour ago to prepare for the reception to be given here tomorrow evening. Unfortunately at this moment, I can't invite you into the grounds to take your pictures, but as we advance with *glasnost,* it may be different in a year's time. Until then . . ."

Not so long ago, my camera would have been ripped from my hands, and I might have been interrogated by the KGB with considerably less grace.

SEVEN

Cultural Circles

GORBACHEV'S APPOINTMENT as General Secretary in 1985 is now universally regarded as a watershed in Soviet history. Sacred cows were slaughtered, obsolete ideas thrown out. Among the more radical changes were those initiated on behalf of Raisa. Not only was she the first First Lady, she became a salaried one. Now, the wife of the General Secretary appeared on the list of paid officials of the Presidium of the Supreme Soviet. Her responsibilities: to advise on matters of protocol, social issues, and questions pertaining to women and work—duties sufficiently vague so as to make her authority commensurately vague. For this, she was given several hundred rubles a month and a Volga (in addition to the Chaika she already had as the General Secretary's wife).

But her paid responsibilities did not end there. Not long after Gorbachev's promotion, she was appointed vice president of the Soviet Cultural Foundation, an organization with the aim of promoting and conserving

Soviet art. There she worked with her father's former cellmate, the esteemed Dmitri Likhachev, the president of the foundation, with whom she had a special rapport, despite the minor scandal that marked their early days. Though Likhachev's position was honorary, Raisa's, as stipulated by foundation bylaws, was not, and she received a salary of several hundred rubles a month. On learning this, the public was incensed. As wife of the General Secretary, they believed she already had enough privileges, not to mention income. Consequently, the salary was withdrawn and the position converted to "honorary." None of this affected her work with Likhachev. As he had her father, he imbued her with the belief that the peoples of the Soviet Union had a right to their own ethnic cultures and that history should be presented in true and non-propagandist terms. Likhachev's theories became her creed; "The Russian soul needs freedom."

The foundation has its headquarters in a splendid building that, before the Revolution, was owned by the Tretyakov family (as in Tretyakov Gallery, which houses a famous collection of Russian art). But after the Revolution, the building fell into the hands of the Ministry of Defense, which used it as a place to entertain guests. Only with great reluctance did the powerful ministry give it over to the foundation. Raisa supervises the upkeep of the building, as well as working conditions of the staff, with meticulous care. Guests are received in the large and gracious Oak Room on the first floor and treated to Indian tea, caviar, and other delicacies out of the reach of ordinary Soviet citizens.

Committee meetings at the foundation are long and sometimes controversial. Among the more unpopular suggestions raised at one meeting was Raisa's motion that they cut both salaries and the size of the paid staff. Predictably, people balked. They complained not only how easy it was for someone as well off as Raisa to preach austerity, but how tactless, even vengeful, in light of her own recent demotion from "paid" to "honorary" status. Nonetheless, she justified her plea in ringingly patriotic terms. "The time has not yet come when we can freely pay such high salaries. We must work harder and do more for our country."

Aside from Likhachev, Raisa has two other close associates at the foundation: George Myasnikov, its executive chairman, and Ivetta Voronova, the fund-raising chief. Voronova arranges benefit performances, concerts, and exhibitions for the foundation (many of which the Gorbachevs cannot attend because of their busy schedule). The administrative work of the foundation takes up much of Raisa's time. Meetings of the governing committee can last from ten or eleven in the morning to three or four in the afternoon, with only two short breaks for refreshments. These, Raisa spends in the executive chairman's office since, as vice president, she doesn't have her own. Still, deference is paid. On days when the governing committee formally meets, Myasnikov receives Raisa at the foot of the stairs and escorts her to the Oak Room.

And, naturally, it's Vice President Raisa whom overseas guests clamor to see, though not many succeed. Exceptions are generous donors, such as Baron Heinrich Thyssen-Bornemisza, who presented to the foundation his *Landscape with Figure,* a work by the late seventeenth- and early eighteenth-century Italian painter Allessandro Magnasco (his paintings appear in galleries in Moscow and Leningrad). *Landscape* now hangs in the Pushkin Fine Art Museum in Moscow. In thanking the baron, Raisa sounded her usual doctrinaire note: "The exchange of works of art brings mutual enrichment and promotes international understanding."

Another person honored by the foundation was Armand Hammer, one of the Soviet Union's oldest friends and certainly, till recent times, among its few capitalist ones. In 1988, the mega-industrialist was made an honorary member of the foundation (he died in December 1990, at the age of ninety-two). Over the years, Hammer had numerous dealings with the Soviets. During desperate times in the 1920s, he flew grain into Russia in exchange for paintings, which he acquired on extremely favorable terms. These paintings decorated the walls of his luxurious apartment in Moscow, much to the consternation of his critics (who wanted to see them back in the Tretyakov Gallery, where they had hung before the trade). Hammer was the only private citizen from the West who had permission to fly in Soviet airspace without a Russian copilot as navigator.

Even abroad, Raisa continues her work for the foundation. Every gift she receives that has any connection with art, she donates to the foundation. On her return from a state visit to Great Britain in 1989, for example, she brought a portrait of Tsar Peter III. In presenting it, Lord Gowrie, a former minister of the arts, noted, "It is a painting by your Russian artist Alexander Rokotov." "No, it isn't," Raisa said. "It is 'school of Rokotov.' " In any case, the picture now hangs in the Russian Museum in Leningrad.

In return, Raisa gives presents, too. "As a memento of my visit to the Beethoven Museum," she told the director of the museum, in Bonn, West Germany, "I should like to present this manuscript music book, one of the most valuable documents from our Central Museum of Musical Culture in Moscow. Until now, you had four pages from it; we have added 174 more."

As a result of the Cultural Foundation's work, the Soviets now have a role, however modest, in the international art scene. This is partly due to Raisa, but also to Gorbachev's close associate and *Pravda* editor in chief, Ivan Frolov. Through Frolov and his many contacts among Russian-studies experts in the West, Raisa receives catalogs of major art auctions in the West, as well as news of large exhibitions and cultural trends. Frolov's cultural contacts help the Soviets in an even more fundamental way. One of them will occasionally bid incognito for a valuable manuscript or work of art. In this way, the Russians acquired in Baden-Baden in 1989 the letters of Turgenev (for a five-figure sum) and, at Sotheby's in London, an unpublished letter by Pushkin (for £32,000, or about $57,600) and a manuscript of Turgenev's *Fathers and Sons* (£400,000, or $720,000).

Obviously the Cultural Foundation has considerable funds at its disposal. Raisa's main job, however, is not fund-raising, but maintaining this vital international link. Her foundation work, which has grown in recent years, is important to her identity as First Lady as well. Now when she stands beside her husband in public it is not just as his wife, but as a key player in a realm that is not only glamorous and exciting, but has real economic significance to the nation.

The Gorbachevs are passionate theatergoers. Unlike previous Soviet leaders and their wives, who could only be seen at performances of the Bolshoi, or opera or concerts at the Palace of Congresses in the Kremlin, Raisa and Mikhail venture farther afield, to avant-garde theaters like the Taganka, where they are frequently invited backstage. They are especially close with Mikhail Ulyanov, artistic director of the Vakhtangov Theater. Occasionally, they will even take their artistic friends abroad. A large group of performers accompanied them on a recent visit to the United States. These friendships are not without political merit. The artists they befriend and support are goodwill ambassadors for the politics of *perestroika*.

EIGHT

The Gorbachev Partnership

THOUGH LIFE IS COMFORTABLE behind their dacha's walls, there's another side to the Gorbachevs' life: pressure, tension, and work. Like other public officials, they pay a price for their privileges: loss of privacy and autonomy, and criticism from a dissatisfied public and carping press. But maybe this was as Stalin planned it. This Communist paradise could be yours but, in turn, you had to sell your soul to the state. Unlike the corporate executive who earns and therefore owns his luxuries, your dacha, your Chaika, your summer villa are all just magnificent loans.

And for theirs, the Gorbachevs work hard. As First Lady (not to mention wife, mother, grandmother, and supervisor of two households), Raisa keeps to a strict schedule. At 6:00 A.M., she and her husband are awoken by their staff. No matter how tired (or terrific) they feel, a medical checkup is mandatory. Even before they get out of bed, their blood pressure is taken (by Irina or her husband Anatoly, also a doctor, if they are in the house).

Afterward, Raisa has a short swim, a glass of fruit juice, and then breakfast with Mikhail. The menu is typically Russian: porridge, curd cheese, bacon omelets, Kefir (yogurt), and coffee or tea (the Gorbachevs prefer German coffee and English tea).

They discuss their schedules, then Mikhail goes off to his Central Committee office, a forty-minute drive. (If at any time Raisa needs to speak to Mikhail, she can reach him via the state security line, though nonemergency use is frowned upon.) She stays home to complete her domestic chores. Usually, they take an hour, during which she reviews the day's menus with the chef, consults with the housekeeper, pays bills, and orders food.

Next, she turns to the mail. Hundreds of letters arrive each day addressed to both Raisa and Mikhail. Those from abroad are sent first to a special department of the Central Committee where they are read and analyzed, their contents written up in comprehensive reports. Which letters actually reach the Gorbachevs is decided by their personal staff. Letters on women's issues are sent directly to Raisa, who as a rule spends no less than two hours a day on the mail. Both she and Mikhail regard these letters as invaluable—their pipeline to the real world. Raisa, who pays closer attention to the mail, summarizes the letters that should be brought to Mikhail's notice. In addition to letters, she reads newspapers and magazines, and at least skims a few new books a day. She is Gorbachev's unofficial press officer. He has official ones, too, but none who outdoes his wife's scrupulous briefings.

By the time Raisa finishes her paperwork, it's two o'clock, time for lunch in the dacha and elsewhere throughout Russia. Lunch in the Soviet Union is a later meal than it is in America; larger, too. It might consist of juice, salad, or fish as an appetizer; soup (borscht with lemon and sour cream, a cream of vegetable or, in summer, Raisa's favorite, okroshka, a chilled soup made of diced meat, vegetables, and herbs, perked up with kvass); a main course of chicken or lamb (Mikhail is partial to vegetable casseroles and curries); and for dessert, fresh fruit. High-calorie desserts are generally forbidden: Raisa keeps a vigilant watch on her figure.

After lunch, if her schedule allows, she rests (lunch in Russia is obviously an ordeal). Otherwise, it's on to meetings, sometimes two and three a day with various figures in culture and the arts. On lighter days, when she has no meetings and can remain at the dacha, she has a late-afternoon snack: fruit, curd cheese, honey and milk, supposedly to maintain her smooth, porcelain skin.

Mikhail seldom arrives home before nine o'clock, but Raisa always waits to dine with him. Dinner is a lighter meal than lunch: salad, fish (they like sturgeon, trout, pike, and perch), and, for dessert, perhaps a compote of curd cheese, raisins, and dried apricots or, their only treat, small cherry-filled pastries. Like Cossacks, they eat little bread and not much meat or potatoes. Neither likes highly spiced food. Once or twice a week, food from the West is delivered, usually seafood, and Mikhail loves French cheeses.

After dinner, they walk in their garden, discussing the day's events, its victories and problems, or go out to the theater, though never on impulse. Such expeditions require a major fuss, at least in security terms. Auditorium entrances must be checked, the street in front of the theater cleared to make way for the Gorbachevs and their fleet of Zils. Once inside, they are ushered into a special box reserved for the Kremlin chief and his family. All state theaters, whether the Bolshoi, Palace of Congresses, or lesser-known ones, have boxes reserved exclusively for the chief. Even theaters Gorbachev never attends have boxes reserved for him, which is why there are empty theater boxes all over Moscow, in addition to empty apartments, dachas, and hospital rooms reserved for the elite. And what a shame to waste such views.

Most of the boxes are balcony level, stage left, except at the Bolshoi, where the so-called tsar's box affords an even better view, at orchestra level and directly in front of the stage. Stage right is a director's box, reserved for visiting dignitaries or friends of the house. But the comforts extend beyond just the view. To the rear of the General Secretary's box are two richly furnished rooms, complete with a buffet. Should Gorbachev come directly from Central Committee headquarters, which he often does, he can dine between acts.

The Gorbachevs rarely go to the theater alone. With them in their box is at least one security guard and sometimes friends, Eduard Shevardnadze and his wife or the Medvedevs (Vadim Medvedev is the Politburo's ideology man). After the performance, the waiting convoy of Zils whisks them back home.

For most of the year, Raisa and Mikhail, like most working couples, see each other only at night, which is why public holidays, weekends, and the four weeks they regularly spend in Pitsunda, a beautiful old Georgian town on the Black Sea, are such a treat. Here they can rest, recharge and, mostly, be alone. A photograph taken outside their summer house shows a laughing Raisa, hiding from the sun behind an umbrella. The Gorbachevs had planned to acquire a newer holiday home in nearby Miyussera; a leading architect from Tbilisi had already been hired to design it in the Byzantine style. But the Congress of People's Deputies vetoed the project—the people are opposed to such ostentation, it declared—and the project was scrapped. Raisa reportedly was miffed.

She and Mikhail also spend more time together during their official trips, whether in Russia or abroad. Protocol limits how often and in what capacity she appears with him, but since her husband's accession, the rigid protocol of the past has been relaxed. Even on her own, though, Raisa apparently enjoys herself. While intensely involved in Gorbachev's activities, she generates her own, and in doing so, wins plaudits from the international press.

Time with friends is the only thing missing from the Gorbachevs' schedule. This may be by choice—as a couple, they are extremely symbiotic—or merely the result of the demands imposed on them. Preoccupied from morning to night with affairs of state, Gorbachev hardly has time for friends, at least not those outside the political realm. One exception is the crowd at his annual birthday bash, held each year at the dacha. Among the guests is Yuri Stupin, a friend from Stavropol days who now, thanks to Gorbachev, is director of the office responsible for allocating resort facilities to state trade unions, and Alexander Vlasov, a former minister of the interior and a friend for more than fifteen years. Shevardnadze and his wife are usually there. When Gorbachev first suggested him for the foreign minister's post, Shevardnadze expressed doubt that he could handle the job, which Gorbachev quickly dismissed. "We've decided already," he said. Some family members are also there, but others are conspicuously absent. Though showing none of the propensity for scandal of some of the famous political families in the West, the Gorbachevs, too, have their family heartaches.

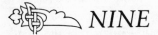 *NINE*

Family Ties

As a NUCLEAR FAMILY, the Gorbachevs are extremely close. Their extended-family ties are less strong. Mikhail stays in touch with his cousin and childhood friend, Fedya Rudchenko, also a guest at the annual birthday party. Mikhail and Raisa are close not only to Rudchenko, sixty-two, but to his wife Galina and their daughter, Xenia, a criminologist with the Stavropol militia. Relations are less cordial with Mikhail's younger brother, Alexander Gorbachev, forty-one, a colonel on the General Staff. Alexander, known as Sasha, an enthusiastic guitarist, is married and has a daughter, Lena (a student at the No. 2 Medical Institute in Moscow, where Irina worked). Observers attribute the coolness to the fact that Sasha is only Mikhail's half-brother, but perhaps it's because Raisa does not get along with either her brother-in-law or his wife.

She is, however, close to Mikhail's mother. Maria Gorbachev is in many ways the archetypal Russian mother, a woman of strong will who does what she wants. While Mikhail and Raisa were away, she reportedly had her granddaughter Irina baptized secretly, seeing the christening as her duty to God. She is not afraid to speak her mind and, over the years, has given her son several pieces of advice, including: "If you have a head full of troubles, go into the field and work them off. That's the way to see things straight." Another, and one he finds easier to heed: "Listen to Raisa, take her advice. She wants the best for you."

Maria Gorbachev still does farm chores in Privolnoye, where she keeps pigs and chickens. Her neighbors regard her as an honest soul; even when people want to do her favors as mother of the General Secretary, bring her sugar and other supplies, she refuses and insists on doing all her shopping at the village market. She is a Christian and will remain one until the day she dies, she says. And she refuses to move to heathen Moscow. "So they can cremate me there?" she jokes. (In the country, the dead are buried; in urbane Moscow, cremation is preferred.)

Some people say that Maria Gorbachev is closer to Sasha than to Mikhail. Once there was a fierce family row over where she would live. Sasha wanted her to live with him and his family in Odintsovo, some twenty minutes from Moscow. But Mikhail insisted that if she wouldn't come to Moscow to live with him, then she would remain in Privolnoye. She still lives in a modest cottage built with financial help Mikhail gave her while his father was still alive. But privacy is no longer her privilege. Security around her house has been stepped up following threats by Azerbaijani extremists to wipe out the entire Gorbachev clan. Should a Western visitor wish to take a closer look at Privolnoye, he can't. It's out of bounds for foreigners.

Raisa remains close to her mother, "Baba Shura," as she is called. Since the death of her husband, who died of throat cancer in 1986, Shura has lived as a pensioner in Krasnodar. She has a small apartment in a five-story building built in Khrushchev's time (the "Khrushchovka"), which was allotted to Maxim Titorenko when he retired from the railroad. Shura frequently visits her daughter in Moscow, and Raisa travels regularly to Krasnodar. Also for security reasons, Krasnodar is off-limits to foreigners.

As a grandmother, Raisa herself, it turns out, is fairly traditional, that is, smitten by her two granddaughters. Anastasia, the younger, looks like Mikhail. She is only four, so not much is known about her (except that her favorite toy is a blue and pink furry elephant her grandmother brought her from Paris). About Xenia, born in 1979, more is known: She attends Moscow Special School No. 4, where English is the second language, and in her free time attends the Choreographic School of the Bolshoi Theater. There, she studies under the famous Galaptina, who teaches the children of the elite. When possible, Raisa picks up Xenia at class, sometimes stopping to discuss her progress with the principal, and then whisks her home in the family Zil.

Like her mother, Irina was a gold-medal student, and followed in her mother's footsteps in matters of romance as well: she married a Stavropol boy. But unlike Mikhail, Irina's husband, Anatoly Verganski, is from a professional family: his mother is a neuropathologist at the No. 8 Polyclinic in Stavropol (his father died of a brain tumor when Anatoly was still young). Anatoly and his brother are both trained as heart surgeons (they have less status in Russia than in the West), and he and Irina were students at the Medical Institute together.

Raisa was pleased with, and apparently not uninvolved in, Irina's choice of mate. Once Raisa made up her mind which of Irina's suitors she preferred, none but Anatoly was allowed inside the Gorbachev house. "I'm glad my daughter didn't fall for a playboy from the city," she has said. Irina and Anatoly were married in

1977, in a far more lavish ceremony than her parents had. White Volgas ferried the wedding guests from here to there during the two-day festivities (one for the official ceremony and official guests; the other for parties with friends). The wedding breakfast was at the Gorka Restaurant, quite a step up from the student dining hall where Raisa, Mikhail, and their revelers were happy to have sausage and tea. A wedding photo, taken as the ring was being slipped on Irina's finger, shows a couple who appear very happy and very young. Rumor has it that Mikhail drank more than a few toasts with the porter, but it is hard to imagine such non-nomenklatura behavior, especially with Raisa looking on.

Irina brings to the marriage all the virtues of a dutiful daughter, at least from the traditional Russian point of view. She is well educated and knows how to cook, bake, sew, and knit, thanks to Yefremova, one of the family servants. She also plays the piano, speaks fluent English and, not surprisingly, is knowledgeable about art. People admire her, the product of an apparently felicitous match between a strong and stimulating mother and a father who, despite his ambition, has a warm and fatherly heart.

Until Anastasia was born, Irina worked as a lecturer at the No. 2 Medical Institute in Moscow. At the time, her husband was an assistant surgeon at the Gradski Hospital, whose director, Victor Savelyev, is a specialist in heart surgery and whose wife is Raisa's gynecologist. For Soviet women, seeing a gynecologist is rare; seeing one once a year, rarer yet. Attitudes toward women's health are still primitive, at best. Gynecological treatment in particular is minimal, partly because of inadequate facilities and partly because of the refusal of many men to allow their wives to be examined so intimately by a stranger. As a result, many women suffer illness and unwanted pregnancies. Abortion in the Soviet Union, in general, is a nightmare, performed without anesthesia and using outmoded procedures that boost the mortality rate. But women's suffering, viewed as holy and/or trivial, doesn't seem to interest men. Nor do their feelings about childrearing. Family planning is women's business, they say. Hence the high abortion rate, since the state health care system does not give out contraceptives.

Raisa's relations with other family members are strained. All through college, Raisa kept in touch with her brother, Evgeny, and her sister, Ludmilla, but not anymore. Ludmilla is a doctor married to an engineer. She has two children, a daughter at the Academy of Art in Moscow who hopes to be an artist, and a son at the Technical High School in Moscow, but the marriage appears to be foundering. Ludmilla practices in Ufa, a city in the southern Urals best known for being the most polluted in Russia. Whether for geographic or other reasons, the sisters rarely meet.

Evgeny's story is even sadder. After military training, he studied philosophy at Moscow State, but after that his path diverged from Raisa's. He married twice (his son did military service in East Germany) and was a writer of children's stories and novels, none of which was published. "His stories have a touch of Kafka," Raisa once said. One of then, "Kitomski's Sea," written in 1973, depicts a sailor stationed in a North Sea port who comes home on leave, falls in love, and marries. After the wedding, he goes back north to prepare a house for his bride. On the day of her arrival, he waits onshore as her ship comes into the harbor. And here the tragedy is more bathetic than Kafkaesque: seeing a mine, he dives in, defuses it to save his love but loses his life.

For years Evgeny has lived alone in Voronezh. He has a drinking problem and apparently underwent a cure in a psychiatric clinic in Orel. When he has too much to drink, he allegedly verbally abuses his famous sister. Undoubtedly, Evgeny's situation was behind Raisa's urging her husband to launch an anti-alcohol campaign at a time when consumption of vodka in the Soviet Union had reached alarming heights. Except on rare occasions, Raisa doesn't drink and is vehemently opposed to alcohol.

Maxim Titorenko died in the summer of 1986. Almost all of his family assembled for the funeral. Mikhail placed a bunch of red carnations beside his portrait. Raisa, carrying a spray of roses, supported her grieving mother, but her face, too, was wracked with pain. In the typical Soviet style, Titorenko, shrouded in white, lay in an open coffin surrounded by candles. Evgeny and Ludmilla were also there, in addition to Irina, Anatoly, his mother, and Raisa's friend Lydia Budyka and her husband. There was also a group of more colorfully dressed mourners—Maxim's relatives from the Ukraine.

TEN

The Woman
and Her Clothes

COMPARED TO NANCY REAGAN or Jacqueline Onassis or Daniele Mitterrand, Raisa is hardly the embodiment of chic. But compared to her predecessors and her countrywomen generally, with their garish makeup and shoddily made clothes, she is indeed a fashion queen. And for this she receives both criticism and praise—and, always, lots of press. "Raisa has fifty couture dresses from Paris designers," one newspaper will blare. "Each of her outfits costs at least £3,000," trumpets another. "Raisa is a walking advertisement for Cardin or Yves Saint Laurent" (not a compliment in the USSR).

Russian women are so interested in Raisa's wardrobe because she's one of the few Russian women who has one. And where else can they see such well-made clothes? Not in Italian or French fashion magazines, which aren't available at the local kiosk, nor in Soviet stores with their pathetic stock of flimsy goods. Consequently, people study Raisa, and offer their opinions.

Some praise her understated elegance, pronounce the mixture of stripes, dots, and diamonds in the material of her English-style suit just right. Others, more sophisticated, are also less kind. Karl Lagerfeld, for example, thought the gold thread in one outfit better suited for a beer garden than a state visit. You couldn't say she owns "fashions," he said, merely a wardrobe full of clothes. But even her harsher critics agree: her clothes are a major improvement over her predecessors'. And besides, whatever she wears, she looks good.

Slava Zaitsev, a celebrated Soviet designer whose avant-garde fashions have even been written about in the West, does not count Raisa among his clients. "We are perhaps too complicated for each other," he says. Besides, the designer loves white and his sketches seem far too Parisian even for a member of the Moscow elite: lovely, supple bodies in slim, graceful clothes—a touch of Art Nouveau—everything loose, fluent, inventive. Such a man would not be happy designing the typically dark and conservative suit Raisa wears. Nonetheless, based on two events he and Raisa attended, the presentation of the Yves Saint Laurent collection at the French Embassy and opening night of *Sophisticated Lady* in Moscow, he concedes that she has all the raw materials: a well-proportioned, trim figure, slim legs and, most important, the desire to look attractive. He especially admires her hair. "When I was young, I designed clothes for Raisa Gorbachev all the time, without ever telling her," he said. "I was fascinated by her hair. It inspired me, the color, the richness, the possibilities."

That Zaitsev doesn't design clothes for Raisa is partly because he hasn't been asked, but also because he is interested in designing for the masses and not the elite. Asked if he ever designed clothes for Irina, he replied, "I am a couturier, not a celebrity-hunter."

For years, Zaitsev's goal as director of the Institute of Fashion, with its four hundred employees, has been to design a new type of everyday appeal for the general public (an exemplary socialist goal). He finds himself severely constrained by shortages of every sort—fabric, thread, zippers, labor-saving machinery. Surely this must cramp his style? Could Yves Saint Laurent or Lagerfeld work under such conditions? Zaitsev believes he can: "Out of nothing, everything"—a rather sanguine view.

He is even more optimistic post-*perestroika*. "When Gorbachev took over this country, it was in a catastrophic state," Zaitsev said. "He may be only one man, but people in the Soviet Union are already friendlier and more human with each other. That is no small thing." He believes that designing for a woman is a way of improving her life, though the process is far from simple. Only when he has really studied a woman, her height, her posture, her figure, especially her hips—often a problem for Russian women—does he get ideas. "Just imagine if Raisa came in and said, 'Mr. Zaitsev'—she wouldn't say Slava, not Raisa—'I need a dinner dress.' I would have to think about this in a practical way. I would first need to know how much fabric I could use. So often wives of Soviet officials come with the minimum amount of dress material. Possibly they didn't have the foreign currency to buy more, possibly they'd been given the length of fabric as a gift. Shortage of material challenges my powers of invention. For the Tsarina Raisa with her glowing chestnut hair, I would design a straight little black dress, about knee-length, softly tailored, interwoven with pearly threads, worn with glittering black stockings, high heels—that would be my 'Raisa Glasnost' design."

But he is right: it is hard to see Raisa yielding to his technique, which is rather Svengalian. He doesn't want a client who simply orders a dinner dress; he wants ones who come to him and say, "Look at me, Mr. Zaitsev. What can be done with me?" His aim is to create new personalities, not just clothes. But a woman like Raisa is hardly in need of a new persona. And besides, for an artist like Zaitsev, she has too many ideas of her own.

Far better suited to Raisa's temperament and style is someone like Sonya Karotnikova, her dressmaker in Stavropol days. During that period, Karotnikova made dresses not only for Raisa but Irina, too, including her wedding dress. She also designed the dress Raisa wore that day. Reminiscing, Karotnikova said, "While we were trying things on, Mikhail lay down on a couch. He had just come back from an official trip and he had a headache. We fitted the dress on, and I said to Raisa, 'This dress is my wedding present.' Raisa looked wonderful in it, but she said, 'No, it's too expensive a gift.' I insisted she should have it. Otherwise, I said, I would take it back home. At this point, Mikhail opened his eyes and looked fondly at Raisa, saying, "Ah, Sakhar [Sugar], you've never had a dress like that, and how beautiful you look!' " ("Sakhar" is one of Mikhail's pet names for Raisa. "Commissar" is another, dating back to their student days, when Raisa liked to wear Mikhail's leather jacket. Even then, she liked to give orders.)

"He loves her so much," Karotnikova said. "Once, in the late 1960s as I remember, Mikhail went to Italy and spent all his money on silver jewelry to bring back to Raisa. I made her a silver cocktail dress, and she later wore the dress and the jewelry for their silver wedding. She looked marvelous."

Karotnikova was Raisa's friend as well as dressmaker, and one on whom she relied. "Bring me three hundred rubles and I will make you a fantastic dress," the dressmaker would say. Obediently, Raisa would bring the money, leaving Karotnikova free to decide on the fabric and style. "When she was choosing designer clothes, too, I had to decide," Karotnikova said. "She always told me, 'Sonya, you have the last word. Shall I take it or not?' " She recalled a trip the Gorbachevs made for a Communist Party fête in fashion-conscious Italy. When their escort called Raisa "Signora Grazia" (the lady with the graces), Raisa modestly gave all the credit for her appearance to her dressmaker, a compliment the dressmaker returns. "What makes the difference in clothes is the person inside them," Karotnikova said. "Raisa knows how to wear clothes. She makes them come alive."

Today, Raisa's clothing comes from many sources, including catalogs, through which she, like many wives of top Soviet officials, orders copies of Dior, Claude Montana, and Chanel. Another is the annual Festival of Fashion in Moscow. Here, fashion houses from all over the Soviet Union show their clothes. If Raisa sees something she likes, she will often order it straight off the runway. During trips abroad, she almost always finds time to visit couturiers and see fashion shows. In 1986, for example, during a state visit to East Germany, she slipped out to a boutique to buy clothes for herself and Irina. Western countries, delighted by her interest, usually try to accommodate her, arranging their own little summits between Raisa and their fashion czars. Sometimes, they give her clothing, which she usually passes on to Irina. Many of the clothes are too bold, if not for her, then certainly for the jury back home.

In some ways, Raisa's interest in fashion has acted as a tonic on the Soviet clothing industry. And though one woman can hardly make up for the vast gap between what shoppers want and what they can buy, she tries, urging factories to produce more highly styled goods and in greater variety.

Raisa's present dressmaker and fashion mentor is Tamara Makeyeva. In winter, Makeyeva works in the state House of Fashion in Moscow, known for its more conservative approach to color and style. (For many years, Makeyeva shared a studio with Zaitsev, but obviously the two had no effect on each other's work.) In summer, she secludes herself in her private dacha in Kostroma, past the beautiful Russian towns of Rostov, Veliki, and Yaroslavl along the Volga, where even her most famous client cannot call. The designer is proud of the fact that Aleksandr Ostrovsky, the great nineteenth-century Russian dramatist, had his estate in nearby Shilikova. Makeyeva's husband is an actor at the Mossovet Theater in Moscow, which is how she and Raisa met. A few years before Gorbachev became General Secretary, friends from the Mossovet Theater suggested that the actor's wife should design an ensemble for Raisa. The result: a dark blue suit, rather severely cut, with a short jacket, white blouse, and two skirts (one short, one long). Apparently, Raisa liked the suit well enough to call the designer again.

Their sessions, never less than two hours at a time, are always very cozy. Before Raisa arrives, Makeyeva has studied the latest fashion trends in Rome, Paris, and London, though Raisa, of course, will have her own ideas. In general, Makeyeva says, Raisa prefers warm, bright colors—she's very partial to red—and is adamant about coordination: everything must match. Before getting down to business, there is time for chitchat and a little herbal tea, made from black currant, lime flower, and dried mint that Makeyeva collects in the forest around her dacha. When both women have agreed on a design, Makeyeva's assistant cuts the pattern and sews the dress for the first fitting. If Raisa likes it, it makes the short list. If she likes it a lot, she can usually be seen a few days later in a smart new dress.

Naturally, Makeyeva is ecstatic about the effect her client is having on the world. "She is the first General Secretary's wife who dresses well and shows the world how good a Russian woman can look," she says. As for Raisa's impact closer to home, Makeyeva agrees: few Soviet women could emulate Raisa even if they wanted to. Still, she believes that with a little effort, even without the Soviet equivalent of Neiman-Marcus or Saks, Soviet women can improve their wardrobe. "That need not cost a great deal of money," she said. "Small details can make a huge improvement."

As for her own role, Makeyeva is delighted with that, too. To see her clothes alongside those of Cardin, Lagerfeld, and Dior is certainly a thrill for a Soviet designer. In her less humble moments, the sixty-year-old dressmaker imagines her name being mentioned in the same breath with Cardin's and Dior's. Fortunately, she doesn't read Western newspapers or she would be disappointed to see Cardin, Nipon, Lagerfeld, and a host of others, but no Makeeva—at least not yet.

Over the years, Raisa has often brought gifts to her dressmaker—trinkets for Makeyeva's grandchildren and, each year on her birthday, a bouquet from the Kremlin. On the eve of her sixtieth birthday, Madame Makeyeva awaited a larger than usual present. "Raisa's love of giving presents is one of the strongest traits in her character," Makeyeva said.

Raisa's hair and makeup belong in other hands. Several stylists are responsible for her stunning chestnut highlights and glowing complexion. Up until 1985, Boris Gusiyev advised her on makeup and did her hair. At the time, he was working at the Moscow Hair Research Institute, where with the Soviet's love for paperwork, it was the custom for clients to fill out detailed questionnaires, and then for stylists to add their opinions. Why isn't exactly clear, though it was a custom Raisa followed. Gusiyev said the first time she came was with a woman friend, a philosophy professor. Afterward, Raisa came in regularly, two or three times a month. Sometimes she took advice from Gusiyev, sometimes from her other beauty czar (Mikhail, who liked her hair to have a hint of romance about it. For that, a little henna was deployed). Regarding makeup, Gusiyev said, Raisa relied on a good, cream-colored foundation, and unlike the majority of Soviet women, whose lipstick ranges from harsh red to strident purple, she liked delicate rosy pinks.

Raisa and Gusiyev discussed topics other than hairstyle and makeup—not hairdresser gossip but poetry and art, of which Gusiyev was a passionate fan. In talking about Raisa, he quoted from a poem by the famous Russian poet Anna Akhmatova: "The heavens rising into the blue / Are inexhaustible. . . " He then went to his bookshelf and pulled out a slim volume, *Poems of Akhmatova*. "Raisa herself gave me this book as a present," he said. "She also gave me other books of poetry by Akhmatova. We share an enthusiasm for her poetry."

Aside from being a cultured woman, Raisa is "a pleasant and responsive one," Gusiyev said. "She knows what her position demands of her and she is always well groomed. She cares about her appearance, keeps slim and always dresses well. She knows exactly what she wants. She loves to change her hairstyle, sometimes severe, sometimes feminine, but always right for the occasion."

Once, Gusiyev was extremely late for their appointment. He'd been so busy with other clients that he forgot about Raisa. Only the look on her face made him realize what he had done. She didn't chastise him, but his superiors did. At the time, she wasn't the General Secretary's wife, but it was viewed as shameful enough that Gusiyev had inconvenienced the wife of the Central Committee's youngest member.

Gusiyev stopped working for Raisa in 1985 for what he described as "personal reasons" and today is employed in a private hairdressing salon in Moscow, Ginseng, where, he said, he is well paid. Raisa's new hairdresser, Tatiana, is a former colleague of Gusiyev's at the institute. She does Raisa's makeup and accompanies her on trips. But unlike Gusiyev, Tatiana doesn't talk. Upon taking the job, she signed the usual pledge not to say anything about her employer.

Dressmakers, couturiers, and a small slice of Soviet womanhood are excited about their First Lady's accomplishments in the world of style. Others are less impressed.

"Our women are not like her," one Moscow resident said. "I would go crazy with someone like her."

"Why?" he was asked.

"It isn't as if it's her own money she's spending. We have to pay for everything. She ought to wear the kind of cheap stuff we wear, then people in America would realize what's really lacking in Russia."

ELEVEN

The World Stage

BOTH THE GORBACHEVS love to travel, and do well with crowds. During his 1990 visit to the United States, Gorbachev evoked screams reminiscent of Beatlemania, with women shrieking "Gorby! Gorby!" And Raisa, invariably, wins hundreds of inches of print.

Official business takes priority, but on their trips they have personal itineraries, too. "Wherever Raisa goes, she visits art galleries and museums and attends as many concerts and theaters as possible," her friend Lydia Budyka says. "She really enjoys music, books, and paintings, for culture is what impresses her most. She doesn't go shopping. What she brings back are her impressions of a country's culture and its people."

The comments of the loyal Lydia notwithstanding, Raisa does indeed like to shop, but the resentment her purchases have aroused in the past—diamond earrings from Cartier, the alleged American Express Gold Card blitz—has forced her to curb any conspicuous extravagance. The earring incident, a mini-scandal in Russia,

hardly raised an eyebrow anywhere else. During a visit
to London in 1984 (before Gorbachev was General Secretary and Raisa was the subject of bad press), she asked
Margaret Thatcher where she'd bought her lovely diamond earrings. Cartier, Mrs. Thatcher replied, and advised Raisa to insist on a fair price. Newspapers
described the earrings as a charming pair and the price,
$1,700, as altogether reasonable.

That trip, Raisa's international debut, was among her
happiest. Not only was her public charmed, she was,
too, absorbing even the most trivial aspects of Western
behavior and style. With real admiration, she watched
the free and easy way in which the Prime Minister's staff
enlightened her about the official residence. They supplied her with anecdotes, history, even the most trivial
facts (the number of crystals in that splendid crystal
chandelier), and not in a stilted or pedantic way. For
Raisa, the product of an entirely different school, it was
all very thrilling. And since she was not yet First Lady
and her official calendar not so jammed, she had time to
enjoy such moments and let everything sink in.

But after Mikhail became General Secretary in 1985,
such lighthearted diversions were no longer possible.
Not that the press stopped liking her; it was just that
with all eyes on her husband, her behavior inevitably
changed. Once the darling of the British press for her
childlike enthusiasm—jolly, one journalist even called
her—she now became more formal, and as critical reports began to appear in the Soviet (and U.S.) press,
more formal still. Now she had a schedule so full of
official activities and ladies' teas that cultural expeditions or shopping excursions were out, or at least cur-
tailed. Raisa has a habit that perhaps suggests the
anxiety she feels: she pushes her hair back from her
forehead and runs her hand along the nape of her neck—
just making sure there are no loose strands, which there
never are.

Not that there's much room for failure. All trips abroad follow a rigid procedure, virtually every move scripted beforehand. One thing has changed, though, thanks to Gorbachev. Prior to his promotion, Mikhail would enter the plane through the main door and Raisa through a side door out of range of cameras and press. But in 1986, Mikhail did away with this tradition and now he and Raisa board together, for all of Soviet television to see.

For long flights, the Gorbachevs travel in an Ilyushin 62, in a Tupolev for shorter trips. Both are operated by a special department of the Soviet Ministry of Civil Aviation that deals exclusively with Party flights. Two of its fleets of about 25 Ilyushins and 134 Tupolevs are ready, twenty-four hours a day, for any sudden emergency. Like Air Force One, these planes are comfortably appointed with private compartments in which the Gorbachevs can work, eat, and sleep. They also have a conference room that can accommodate about thirty, complete with communications equipment, stenographers' area, and the famous red telephone hotline for nuclear alerts. There are separate cabins for the doctors, security guards, and the mandatory three flight attendants on each trip.

Ten days in advance of the Gorbachevs, security forces arrive in the host country to map routes and plan strategy in cooperation with their host. Five days in advance, Gennady Gerasimov, the chief Soviet spokesman, shows up, along with the Soviet media corps, followed two days later by the chauffeurs and limousines, all of which will be waiting the minute the Gorbachevs touch down. Deplaning with them is an entourage which varies according to the destination. A German-born woman, for example, traveled with the Gorbachevs on their visit to West Germany when resettlement of German-born citizens in Russia was sure to be a major topic of discussion. Directors of principal Soviet museums are often in the group, as well as Raisa's hairdresser and personal aide, the female counterpart to a valet.

Like her husband, Raisa has her own swarm of security men—seven or eight officers from the KGB's Group 5 who are never more than a few feet away. According to the rules, Raisa and Mikhail are not supposed to do anything unexpected, but occasionally they do. Mikhail, for example, likes to schmooze with journalists and mingle with the crowd, which, needless to say, puts the security details of both countries on edge.

In the years since Mikhail became General Secretary in 1985, he and Raisa have visited more than thirty foreign countries, inspiring a number of jokes back home, not all of them friendly. In one, which circulated after a 1989 trip to East Germany that some Russians felt followed too closely on the heels of a punishing session of the Congress of People's Deputies, a Muscovite asks, "What is the difference between the Moscow Olympics and the Congress of People's Deputies?" (Misha is not only Gorbachev's nickname, but the name of the bear that was the symbol of the Moscow Olympics.) The answer: "At the Olympics, Misha had to be inflated to fly away. At the Congress, Misha inflated himself to fly away." The point being that when the going gets rough, Gorbachev flees.

Another popular joke: Lying in bed on a state visit to France, Mikhail asks Raisa, "Did you ever imagine you would one day be sleeping with the General Secretary?" To which Raisa replies, "Did you ever imagine you would be sleeping with the General Secretary's wife?"

Ironically, in asserting herself, even in championing the cause of her countrywomen, which she often does, Raisa draws flak at home. Her speeches abroad exalt Soviet women for their strength, their forbearance, their double duty as workers, wielding jackhammers, hauling trash, digging ditches, all the while, as the Russians say, keeping an eye on the cooking pot. Raisa reminds the world of the sacrifices Soviet women made during the Great Patriotic War, losing their lives, their loved ones and, in many cases, their chance for a normal family life. She is extremely sensitive to pacifist aims; since it is women who suffer most in war, she often argues, it is women who must try not just to preserve peace, but to instigate it.

Nonetheless, the arrows fly. Some of the sharpest hail from Russian émigrés abroad. They castigate Raisa for flourishing while her countrywomen do not. The status of women, they complain, is still unequal (except in the realm of physical labor, where women are given an equal opportunity to break their backs). And so their comments are often malicious: "Raisa likes to ride the gravy train."

Another source of bad press is Raisa's pedantry. In many ways nouveau riche, she flaunts her education, the source of her upward mobility, as another arriviste might flaunt her jewels. In Iceland, Dr. Raisa lectured on the novelist Halldór Laxness, winner of the 1955 Nobel Prize in Literature; in England and America, her press officers issued her opinions of Charles Dickens and J. D. Salinger (even though nobody asked); in France, at exhibitions of Monet, Renoir, and van Gogh, she gave little sermons on the artists and their significance—just what the French needed. Less offensive was her comment on Picasso; she said the Soviets have taken his dove of peace to heart, which struck a sympathetic chord. Having lost 14 to 20 million people in the "Great Patriotic War," few Russians of Raisa's generation think there is anything "great" about even "patriotic" wars. It is an aspect of the Russian soul that Americans rarely see.

Clearly, Raisa doesn't believe in downplaying her intellect, and this has made her a few enemies; in the most notorious instance, Nancy Reagan. People say the former First Lady still smarts from the battery of questions Mrs. Gorbachev asked and Mrs. Reagan couldn't answer during their by-now infamous White House tour. In *My Turn*, Mrs. Reagan makes no secret of her hostility for Raisa: "When she came to tea in Geneva that first day, she struck me as a woman who expected to be deferred to. When she didn't like the chair she was seated in, she snapped her fingers to summon her KGB guards, who promptly moved her to another chair. After sitting in the new spot for a couple of minutes, she decided she didn't like that one either, so she snapped her fingers and they moved her again. I couldn't believe it. I had met first ladies, princesses and queens, but I had never seen anybody act this way."

But their difficulties preceded both the Washington and Geneva summits. At the hastily arranged summit meeting in Reykjavik, Nancy Reagan didn't show up, assuming it was to be strictly business between the two heads of state. But Raisa did, and proceeded not only to steal the show, but to score a few points for the home team. On Nancy's absence, she said, "Perhaps she isn't well, or perhaps she has something else to do." This barbed remark reportedly made Mrs. Reagan's blood boil.

To everyone's relief, Raisa gets along a lot better with Barbara Bush. As is often observed, with Mrs. Bush, she seems softer. Recipes, dogs—whatever interests Barbara, Raisa will discuss. She doesn't seem to feel the competition she did with Nancy. Not that she isn't still Raisa. In Malta, for example, in 1989, America's First Lady stayed home while Raisa showed up. At first, she remained in the background, but not for long. In Soviet diplomatic circles it was said that she listened in an adjoining room to the negotiations between her husband and President Bush so that she could advise Mikhail on the follow-up talks. (Had she been Gorbachev's brother or nephew, would anyone object? And didn't the author of *My Turn* defend her own right to be her husband's behind-the-scenes chief of staff?)

Visiting the Pope in December 1989, Raisa again broke with convention. In contrast to Nancy Reagan and Lady Diana, she arrived for the papal audience without the customary black mantilla and, even more glaring, in a bright red suit (red for Communism). Defending her, Gorbachev said, "She is the atheist of the two of us, but she speaks of the Pope with great reverence, and admits that the radiance of his personality fascinated her greatly, something she did not expect."

At home, her image continues to darken. While her husband is perpetually immersed in crises, Raisa stands beside him in public, a bit too comfortable, perhaps, in sable or mink. And when he argues passionately with male workers, she similarly engages the women around her. Whether in doing so she helps or hinders him is not easy to say. In the short run, the verdict seems to be that she is hurting him. At times, her audience seems determined to criticize her, no matter how inconsequential the presumed offense. During their 1989 visit to Finland, one of the stops the Gorbachevs made was to a school. In a broadcast televised in Russia, Raisa asked the children, who had been studying the language for only two weeks, what they could say in Russian. Some Soviets reacted crossly to the interchange. "They're not robots," one detractor said.

In terms of the press, the honeymoon was over after Geneva, when, in making her debut, she stole the show from even the charismatic Gorby. But as he continued to establish himself as a catalyst for change in world politics, the focus on Raisa continued to grow. Even the Soviet press, which had barely acknowledged her as more than a wife, took its cue from the West and, after 1985, started to portray the Gorbachevs as a team. (The Eastern bloc was slow to catch on. There, she was still photographed walking a step or two behind Mikhail, not quite as First Lady, but a slightly newer-model wife.)

At the summit meeting in Washington in 1987, the Gorbachevs were staying at the Soviet Embassy, heavily guarded by the CIA, while the main Soviet delegation, including Eduard Shevardnadze and his wife, stayed at the Madison Hotel. Raisa decided to give a small reception at the embassy for Russians living abroad, and I was fortunate enough to attend. I had only just entered the reception room when security officers moved me back, conveniently close to the door through which Raisa would enter. She came in wearing her favorite red Makeyeva dress and smiled at me. Noticing that I was pregnant, she asked me when the baby was due. Our conversation moved easily from the common ground of Pushkin to her love of nature and my personal hope that *perestroika* would make life simpler for journalists stationed in the USSR. Partly as a joke and partly as a friendly gesture, I handed her a badge that said "I like Gorby." She smiled but refused to be photographed wearing it. She shook my hand warmly and wished me success in my work.

I saw her up close again during the Gorbachevs' trip to Cuba in April 1989. She arrived wearing a pale blue dress (also designed by Makeyeva) and came down the aircraft gangway bare-legged, which was unusual but eminently sensible, given the heat in Havana (it had been snowing back in Moscow). Evidently, she does not travel light. On the luggage cart were a white hatbox, nine plastic clothes bags, and five leather suitcases. The Gorbachevs stayed in Lajito, the country house of a former film producer dispossessed by the Cuban government. For their visit, new king-size beds were imported from Costa Rica, especially for them.

A high point of the visit was a trip to the onetime home of Ernest Hemingway, now a Hemingway museum. When Raisa was asked as she toured the house whether she had read any Hemingway, she looked aghast. "Who hasn't?" her look seemed to imply. Goaded by her manner, one American journalist asked if she agreed with Hemingway's view of women as wives and mistresses and nothing more. She turned to the reporter and responded acidly, "There are some questions that are so crass they are not worth answering." Her mood—and apparently her opinion—changed by the time she signed out in the visitors' book. "I am happy that I have been able to visit the house where the great writer and humanist Hemingway lived and worked," she wrote.

Word spread among the press that Raisa also wanted to visit the Mochito Bar, where Hemingway had spent a good deal of his time (the "Hemingway cocktail" is named for him), but the visit was vetoed on security grounds. Rumor had it that Raisa consoled herself with a Hemingway cocktail at the villa, but given her strong antipathy to drink, this was probably a little Hemingway-inspired fiction by an overzealous press. Or maybe we journalists had just had too many Mochitos ourselves.

One of Raisa's stops was a government-run children's home, whose occupants, little girls under six, were thrilled with their visitor. Outside, a small group of Young Pioneers greeted her with poetry. Perhaps it made her think of her own childhood as a Pioneer. In return, Raisa said how pleased she was to be there and shook many little hands. They gave her chocolates and a rose; she distributed Russian dolls. Inside, the rooms were brightly decorated and the girls in their Sunday best. A Cuban journalist said bitterly to his neighbor, "Things will all return to normal tomorrow. As soon as Raisa's back is turned, the children will be back in their usual squalor." Before she left, Raisa peeked in on some of the younger wards of the institution, which takes babies as young as six weeks. With her usual concern for children, she insisted that the press keep out so as not to disturb them.

On the last day of her visit, journalists waited in vain for Raisa to show up at the Museum of Fine Arts, as their schedules said she would. Raisa had decided to visit the Museum of the Revolution instead, without the press. These sudden alterations in her program were not uncommon. She has been known to cut short or even cancel appointments abruptly, saying, "That's it. Finished. I'm tired." Naturally, this creates problems for journalists and ruffles the feathers of her hosts. Some German diplomats have complained that the most difficult part of planning a Gorbachev visit was planning for Raisa, who always had her own ideas. Not that they weren't reasonable ones. When the Germans proposed a fashion show of ready-to-wear clothing in Düsseldorf, her answer was *nyet*. She had already gotten enough heat in the Soviet press on this count, and from then on, shopping and fashion shows were out.

My last glimpse of Raisa in public were between October 5 and 8, 1989, during her trip to East Berlin. There, she stayed in the Schloss Niederschönhausen in the Pankov district, and on her last day visited the Zeiss Planetarium. In contrast to her previous visits to East Germany, there were no cheering crowds. Except for a few Young Pioneers and girls from the Communist Youth Organization, security men had discouraged idle spectators from the cavalcade of limousines, whose destination had not been announced.

Among the group greeting her at the planetarium was an East German factory worker who, looking slightly embarrassed with his offering of wilted roses, said that he admired Raisa and that she looked like his wife, who was Russian. He hoped the Gorbachevs will bring *glasnost* and *perestroika* to East Germany, he added. Also in the crowd was a mother carrying a ten-month-old who managed to push through to Raisa. When the baby stretched out her hand, Raisa asked, "Would you let me hold you for a minute?" But the baby had other ideas; she was grabbing at Raisa's black crocodile handbag. "Come, my little diplomat, let's see what your aunt from

Moscow has brought you," Raisa said. She then tried to wrest from her purse a package of pralines. The baby reminded her of her granddaughter Anastasia, she said, who also liked to grab. Raisa gave her handbag to the planetarium director, but still the baby wouldn't let go. "Our little diplomat is never satisfied," she cooed. "Let's look in the bag again and see if we can find something to play with." But at this point, the security guard seemed to signal, "Enough baby. Time to move on."

Before leaving, Raisa told her well-wishers that she was especially pleased that the East Germans seemed so fond of her husband, and that she hoped *glasnost* and *perestroika* would soon be established in their country and make more visits possible. Only the factory worker, still holding his wilted roses, looked disappointed; security guards had prevented him from presenting his offering to Raisa.

But even greater change was on the way. Within weeks the Berlin Wall came tumbling down, and within a year East Germany had ceased to exist.

THROUGH HER JOURNEYS, the many abroad and the long and arduous one from Vessola-yarsk to Moscow, Raisa Gorbachev has learned a great deal. Her English has improved and she has become more savvy in her dealings with the press—she can smile on command and perform other media tricks. Perhaps she will never be quite as warm and spontaneous as she was back in London during 1984 when, before her husband became General Secretary, a British journalist was inspired to call her "jolly" (what a word for the woman the world now sees as impressive, intelligent, strong-willed—definitely not the "jolly" type). In time, under the relentless scrutiny of the press, she will undoubtedly become more self-protective, more cautious, but because she is Raisa, will probably still stray from the traditional path.

Through the media, the world has seen how the wife of the Soviet leader, a lecturer in philosophy, has developed into a woman who moves confidently on the international stage. For all the criticism—and what public figure has not been the victim at one time or another of a judgment-rendering press—she has managed to cut an imposing figure in the world. She smiles and scolds, lectures and pontificates, makes charming, girlish gestures with her hands and gets visibly annoyed. People especially like her habit of reaching out to touch those nearest her, lightly but deliberately, with as much meaning as a quick, official gesture can impart.

No matter what the final verdict, one fact will remain: Raisa Gorbachev has achieved a place in the world, and not just as her husband's wife.

Index

ABOUT THE AUTHOR

URDA JÜRGENS is a freelance journalist based in Moscow. She has traveled widely in the U.S.S.R. and many eastern European countries and has accompanied the Gorbachevs on all their major trips abroad, including the summit meetings in Geneva, Reykjavik, Washington, and Malta.